Series/Number 07-139

CORRELATION
Parametric and Nonparametric Measures

PETER Y. CHEN
Colorado State University

PAULA M. POPOVICH
Ohio University

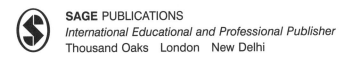

SAGE PUBLICATIONS
International Educational and Professional Publisher
Thousand Oaks   London   New Delhi

For information:

Sage Publications, Inc.
2455 Teller Road
Thousand Oaks, California 91320
E-mail: order@sagepub.com

Sage Publications Ltd.
6 Bonhill Street
London EC2A 4PU
United Kingdom

Sage Publications India Pvt. Ltd.
M-32 Market
Greater Kailash I
New Delhi 110 048 India

Printed in the United States of America

Library of Congress Cataloging-in-Publication Data

Chen, Peter Y. and Popovich, Paula M.
    Correlation: Parametric and Nonparametric Measures / by Peter Y. Chen and Paula M. Popovich.
        p.   cm. – (Quantitative applications in the social sciences; 07-139)
        Includes bibliographical references.
        ISBN 0-7619-2228-8 (p)
        1. Correlation (Statistics) I. Popovich, Paula M. II. Title. III.
        Sage university papers series. Quantitative applications in the social sciences ; no. 07-139
    QA276 .C4665 2002
    519.5′37–dc21

                                                                        2002005573

This book is printed on acid-free paper.

02   03   04   10   9   8   7   6   5   4   3   2   1

Acquiring Editor:	C. Deborah Laughton
Editorial Assistant:	Veronica Novak
Production Editor:	Diana E. Axelsen
Typesetter:	Technical Typesetting Inc.

When citing a university paper, please use the proper form. Remember to cite the Sage University Paper series title and include paper number. One of the following formats can be adapted (depending on the style manual used):

(1) CHEN, P. Y., and POPOVICH, P. M. (2002) *Correlation: Parametric and Nonparametric Measures.* Sage University Papers Series on Quantitative Applications in the Social Sciences, 07-139. Thousand Oaks, CA: Sage.

OR

(2) Chen, P. Y., and Popovich, P. M. (2002). *Correlation: Parametric and Nonparametric Measures.* (Sage University Papers Series on Quantitative Applications in the Social Sciences, series no. 07-139). Thousand Oaks, CA: Sage.

CONTENTS

SERIES EDITOR'S INTRODUCTION

Is there a relationship between variable X and variable Y? This is a central question for the data analyst. The answer comes from examination of the correlation between the two. When high scores of X tend to accompany high scores of Y, the two variables are positively correlated. When low scores of X tend to accompany high scores of Y, the two variables are negatively correlated. Assume, for example, an investigation of academic performance among a random sample of 100 students at State College. Each student is measured on number of hours devoted weekly to homework (variable X) and grade point average (variable Y). Students who put in more hours are found to have a higher GPA, on average. In other words, there is a positive correlation between X and Y.

The temptation of the novice researcher may be to conclude that studying raises GPA. But, before any such conclusion can be reached, the following are some issues to address: (1) What kind of correlation is it? (2) Is the correlation right for the data as measured? (3) Is the correlation statistically significant? (4) How big is the correlation? (5) Is the correlation spurious? In the example, assume that the correlation is the Pearson product-moment correlation, symbolized by the letter r. Given the variables are continuous in their measurement, r is indeed the preferred measure of association. Assume that it is statistically significant at the .05 level. This means studying and grades are quite likely to be related in fact in this population, but it tells nothing about the strength of the relationship. The best assessment of strength is the correlation estimate itself, in this case $r = .45$. Because the theoretical boundaries of Pearson's r go from .00 to 1.00, the relationship appears "moderate," rather than "weak" or "strong."

Does this result allow the conclusion that, at least to some extent, if students study more they will get better grades? Not necessarily. Correlation supports the notion of causation, but it does not prove it. If X does cause Y, then the two will be correlated. But, even if

X and Y covary, one may still not influence the other. There may be some third variable, Z, that is operating on both X and Y to produce the observed correlation. Suppose, for illustration, that Z is academic aptitude. The more academically apt get better grades and study more simply because they like it. Thus, the act of doing the homework itself has little to do with GPA. Of course, this is really only a hypothesis and might be wrong. To test it, the third variable could be controlled for in a partial correlation. On the one hand, if the partial correlation drops to 0, the observed bivariate correlation between X and Y would appear to be causally spurious. On the other hand, if the partial correlation does not budge, the hypothesis of a causal connection between X and Y still cannot be ruled out.

The Pearson product-moment correlation, in pervasive use, is the most important of all measures of association. In this careful monograph by Drs. Chen and Popovich, its calculation and interpretation are fully covered. Important as Pearson's r is, there are many other measures of association, as the bivariate stats options of any current statistical software package reveal. For the beginning analyst, the vast array of possible measures to select from can be bewildering. The Chen–Popovich monograph performs an invaluable service by its systematic organization of the different correlation coefficients.

First, they are organized by level of measurement. In general, level of measurement points to the preferred measure of association. For example, with continuous variables Pearson's r is the measure of choice, whereas for ordinal variables it would probably be a τ, for categorical variables perhaps Cramér's V. Also, they group the measures into parametric and nonparametric. Parametric measures, such as Pearson's r, commonly estimate a population correlation and rest heavily on the assumption of a bivariate normal distribution. Nonparametric measures, in contrast, such as τ_b, have less demanding assumptions. The authors achieve further simplification by demonstrating that several measures of association (e.g., ϕ) are actually just special cases of Pearson's r. After consulting this readable reference, practicing researchers should have considerable confidence in their selection and interpretation of a measure of association.

—*Michael S. Lewis-Beck*
Series Editor

CORRELATION: PARAMETRIC AND NONPARAMETRIC MEASURES

PETER Y. CHEN
Colorado State University

PAULA M. POPOVICH
Ohio University

1. INTRODUCTION

The correlation is probably one of the most widely used, yet also one of the most frequently misused statistics in the natural and behavioral sciences (Carroll, 1961). Arguably, the concept of correlation can be viewed as the foundation of both basic statistics (e.g., *t* test) and advanced statistics (e.g., multivariate analysis of variance), because these other tests either explicitly or implicitly describe relationships or associations among variables of interests.

Suppose we are interested in the relationship between two variables (e.g., driving speed and driving anger). We collect quantitative information on the two variables from the same people, and we can then apply an array of parametric and nonparametric correlation indexes, such as the Pearson product-moment correlation or the Kendall rank-order correlation. All these correlation indexes characterize at least the strength of an association between two variables. In addition to the strength of an association, some correlation indexes can also describe the direction of the relationship. Note that throughout this monograph we will use the word *relationship* to imply both strength and direction, whereas *association* will refer only to the strength.

The ubiquity of the correlation is a function of the fact that there are many ways to describe relationships or associations between variables. If we are interested in the relationships between a set of variables that comprise driving experience, such as driving aggression, driving attention, and driving anger, and another set of variables that

1

characterize driving safety behavior, such as number of traffic citations, collision records, and driving speed, we can gather the above information from the same people and apply canonical correlation statistics. If we are interested in the relationship between one of the driving safety behaviors and a set of variables measuring driving experience, we can apply such statistics as multiple regression or logistic regression.

Correlations, in general, and the Pearson product-moment correlation, in particular, can be used for many purposes in various forms. They can be used (although not limited) to (1) describe a relationship between two variables as a descriptive statistic, (2) examine a relationship between two variables in a population as an inferential statistic, (3) provide various reliability estimates such as test-retest reliability, (4) evaluate validity evidence such as criterion-oriented validation for a psychological inventory, (5) evaluate if one assessment tool or intervention is superior to others (e.g., evaluate if a personnel selection inventory predicts job performance better than other inventories do), (6) gauge the strength of effect, (7) estimate the sample size needed prior to conducting a study, (8) conduct a meta-analytic study, and (9) estimate the utility of an intervention program. Each of the above applications will be discussed in the subsequent chapters. As we will see, these and other correlation techniques can be used to address many topics of interest to both scientists and practitioners across a variety of disciplines.

Characteristics of a Relationship

Relationships or associations between two variables can be measured by correlation indexes (e.g., correlational ratio), which gauge the *strength* of the relationship or association. Generally, we used indexes that range from 0 to 1 in absolute value. The larger the size of the index, the stronger is the relationship between the variables.

Some correlation indexes also describe the *direction* of the relationship. The direction of a relationship can be shown as null, positive, or negative. A null relationship between variables, such as candy consumption and intelligence levels among a group of people, indicates that the variation in candy consumption is not associated with the variation in intelligence for these people. In other words, an increase in candy consumption could be associated with both an increase and a decrease in intelligence, and an increase in intelligence could be associated with both an increase and a decrease in candy consumption.

A positive relationship between variables, such as socioeconomic status and school achievement, suggests that students who have a high socioeconomic status tend to perform well in school. The positive relationship also indicates that students who do not perform well in school tend to have a low socioeconomic status. It is important to note that the positive relationship only reveals that socioeconomic status and school achievement, for some *unsure* reasons, vary together in a similar pattern or the same direction. The positive relationship does not imply in any way that a high socioeconomic status *influences*, *affects*, or *causes* student school performance.

A negative relationship between variables, such as test anxiety and test performance, indicates that students with higher levels of test anxiety have a tendency to perform poorly on tests. This negative relationship also indicates that students are likely to achieve better test performance when they have less test anxiety.

Although the above two examples do seem to imply that socioeconomic status *positively affects* school achievement or that anxiety *negatively impacts* test performance based on *common sense*, these causal conclusions can never be substantiated from the above relationships. This is because the relationships between these pairs of variables may actually be found due to a third variable (a situation that will be described in detail in Chapter 5). For example, the level of preparation prior to a test might affect anxiety toward the test and the test performance. The more time students spend in preparing for tests, the less test anxiety they may experience (i.e., a negative impact). At the same time, test preparation leads to better test performance (a positive impact). The resulting negative relationship between test anxiety and test performance merely reflects the presumed impact of test preparation.

Correlation and Causation

In the previous section, we emphasized that a relationship between two variables does not, and cannot, imply any causal relationship between the variables. As a matter of fact, the distinction between independent variable and dependent variables is not relevant in the correlation context (Hays, 1994). Specifically, neither of the two variables in a correlation should be viewed as an independent or dependent variable. Nevertheless, even though this is often reiterated in statistics or research methods textbooks (e.g., Glass & Hopkins, 1996; Pedhazur & Schmelkin, 1991), the confusion of correlation with causation seems to permeate both research and practice. Let us use a research article published in a medical journal in 2001 as an example. A group of researchers used a longitudinal design to study a hypothesis that there is a relationship between depression (as measured in both 1993 and 1995) and work performance (from self-reported productivity as measured in 1995). They concluded that "depressive disorders in the workplace persist over time and have a major *effect* on work performance" (p. 731, italics added). A director of clinical services who represents a professional association further commented on the result by stating, "The message is clear: There is both medical and financial value in better detection and effective treatment for depression in the workplace." Even though the researchers initially set up the hypothesis pertaining to a *relationship*, they could not help themselves from providing a causal conclusion. Furthermore, the director voiced the need to detect and treat depression based on the rationale that depression *is* at least one of the causes of poor work performance.

Actually, we could also develop an opposite assumed causal direction for this relationship, because it is possible that poor work performance exacerbates depression. Assuming that this causal direction is true, one could then argue that "there is both medical and financial value to improve *work performance* so that *depression* in the workplace can be reduced." This is quite a different strategy from that proposed by the director! However logical either conclusion may seem, it is important to be aware that even if there is a causal relationship between depression and work performance, correlation indexes could not reveal if depression causes poor work performance or if poor work performance causes depression.

There is also the possibility that a third variable could influence both depression and work performance. For instance, the relationship between depression and work productivity might be attributed to the fact that low self-esteem or a poor self-image decrease work performance and increase depression simultaneously. As a result, the negative relationship between work performance and depression appears. Readers can try to generate other plausible explanations for the above relationship between depression and work performance.

Causation is one of the most controversial topics in philosophy and science (Pedhazur & Schmelkin, 1991). Scholars from various disciplines have not (and probably never will) reach a consensus regarding the definition of causation. Nevertheless, Pedhazur and Schmelkin argue that a causal framework is indispensable in research and in practice when we attempt to explain phenomena. James, Mulaik, and Brett (1982) also suggest that an understanding of causation is helpful for us to be able to make inferences.

Based on logical implication (Byerly, 1973), a causal relationship between X and Y can be inferred if (1) effect Y occurs whenever cause X occurs, (2) effect Y never occurs without cause X having already occurred, and (3) effect Y never occurs when cause X has not occurred and effect Y always occurs when cause X has occurred. The previous statement implies that a high correlation should be observed between X and Y (Pearson, 1957). However, even a perfect relationship, such as that between distance and time (assuming the speed is a constant), in no way suggests that time "causes" distance or vice versa. From this, about all that we can safely conclude is that the lack of an association in research probably offers more information regarding the hypothesis of a causal relationship than does the presence of a high correlation (Glass & Hopkins, 1996).

On the other hand, a trivial correlation such as the one between polio vaccine and incidence of paralytic polio in Dr. Jonas Salk's experiment did lead scientists to infer the effect of inactivated polio vaccine (IPV). In Salk's pioneer experiment, there were 201,229 subjects in the control group and 200,745 subjects in the inoculated group. Among those who had received IPV injection, 0.016% later developed paralytic polio. In contrast, there were 0.057% of those in the control group who later developed paralytic polio (data reported in Dowdy & Wearden, 1991). The correlation (based on the phi coefficient described in Chapter 3) between incidence of paralytic polio and IPV injection is a very small -0.01! This is because immunization with IPV triggers a response in the immune system to produce protective antibodies in the blood in most (but not all) IPV recipients.

The above two examples remind us that a perfect positive correlation says nothing about the causality in a relationship. In contrast, a null or trivial correlation does not necessarily imply an absence of causality. In some situations, a negative (or positive) correlation may not rule out a potential positive (or negative) causal relationship (Glass & Hopkins, 1996). For example, suppose there is a negative relationship between sport beverage consumption and weight gain. The more sport beverage that is consumed, the less weight that is gained. A plausible reason less weight is gained can be attributed to lower sugar levels in the sport beverage (which may be replacing the consumption of beverages with higher sugar levels). Consumption of the sport beverage would then actually be an example of a positive causal relationship between sugar consumption and weight gain.

Here is an example that describes how a relationship between variables can be both positive and negative, which further illustrates the complexities involved in interpreting correlations. When rabbits reproduce their offspring every spring, they become primary prey for bobcats. If the secondary prey of bobcats such as mice, voles, and birds are unavailable in some regions, the abundance of rabbits very likely will *increase* bobcat population during this period of time. As a result, a positive relationship between the number of bobcats and the number of rabbits appears. This result could lead a bobcat protection group to conclude that the introduction of bobcats to particular geographical regions does not seem threatening to local rabbit population. However, as time goes on, more bobcats are reproduced and they need more food resources, which threaten the local rabbit population. Consequently, a negative relationship is found. In contrast to the prior conclusion stated by the bobcat protection group, an opposing group would claim that the threat of bobcats to rabbits is a pressing issue.

Yet, how can the relationship between the number of bobcats and the number of rabbits be both positive and negative? As pointed out by Bobko (1995), the answer lies in the dynamic nature of the causal process, which cannot be captured by a correlation. The manifestation of a causal process at a particular time merely reflects an incomplete picture that is easily disguised by different relationships. Most phenomena (if not all) of interest in research or in practice are in essence time dependent, and this should become a relevant factor in the choice of research method.

Correlation and Correlational Methods

By utilizing experimental designs, researchers are often in a much stronger position to infer the cause of a phenomenon, because they can manipulate independent variables and control other extraneous variables (e.g., random assignment, standardization, etc.). Compared to experimental designs, correlational methods tend to limit the ability of researchers to make strong inferences, because researchers have "no control over the presumed antecedents of some phenomenon, and no ability to assign participants at random" (Aronson, Ellsworth, Carlsmith, & Gonzales, 1990, p. 347). Researchers employing correlational methods merely measure variables of interest which are occurring naturally (e.g., density in a department store and shopping behavior, lighting on a highway and driving speed), but do not actually control them for various reasons.

Correlational methods have been widely used to describe any non-experimental methods (e.g., survey or time series). However, the use of correlational methods or correlational studies often creates confusion with the statistical meaning of correlation. Cook and Campbell (1979) have pointed out that "Correlations in the technical statistical sense could be used to analyze data from experiments as well as from nonintrusive observational studies" (p. 295). It is not the statistic that determines whether or not causal conclusions can be reached. It is the rigorous research design and logical reasoning that provide a solid ground for a causal inference. Statistics such as the correlation or other advanced statistics mainly provide us with clues regarding what the plausible causal relationships might be.

Choice of Correlation Indexes

In general, variables studied in the social sciences can be characterized as dichotomous, multichotomous, ordinal, and continuous. Dichotomous and multichotomous variables are also referred to as categorical variables, and they consist of two or more mutually exclusive categories, such as gender, race, political party, or identification number.

In contrast, ordinal variables reflect crude degree or amount of certain attributes of interest. For instance, 50 employees are ranked from 1 to 50 according to their quarterly sales, with 1 standing as the highest and 50 representing the lowest (or vice versa). The actual sales difference between the 1st and the 2nd is most likely different from that between the 49th and the 50th.

Continuous variables gauged at either interval or ratio scales are precise enough to assure the difference between 1 and 2 is the same as that between 49 and 50. Height, amount of charity donation, or blood pressure are just a few examples. Although some would argue

TABLE 1.1

Correlation Indexes

Categorical Variable		Ordinal Variable (3)	Continuous Variable (4)
Dichotomy (1)	Multichotomy (2)		
1 Phi coefficient $\phi^{a,b}$ and tetrachoric coefficient r_{tet}			
2 r_{MD}^{a}	Contingency coefficient C^{b} and Cramér's V coefficient[b]		
3 r_{DR}^{a}	r_{MR}^{a}	Spearman rank-order correlation $r_{rank}^{a,b}$, Kendall's τ^{b} and τ_{b}^{b}, Stuart's τ_{c}^{b}, Goodman and Kruskal's γ^{b}, and Kendall's partial rank-order correlation $\tau_{xy,z}^{b}$	
4 Point-biserial correlation r_{pb}^{a} and biserial coefficient r_{bis}	Eta coefficient η^{a}	r_{RI}^{a}	Pearson's r and first-order partial correlation $r_{xy,z}^{a}$

a. Special cases of Pearson's r.
b. Nonparametric correlation indexes.

that most psychological attributes such as attitude, intelligence, or depression merely reflect ordinal measures, in practice, they are often treated as continuous variables.

According to the above four categories, 10 possible types of relationships between two variables can be created. Although there are many correlation indexes developed to assess the above correspondent relationships, we will focus on 19 parametric and nonparametric correlation indexes in this monograph. These widely used correlation indexes are presented in Table 1.1 and will be discussed in the following chapters.

The distinction between parametric and nonparametric mainly results from whether population parameters (e.g., population correlation, ρ) are estimated, as well as whether certain assumptions (e.g., bivariate normal distribution) are met. In general, a nonparametric correlation requires fewer assumptions and does not attempt to estimate population parameters.

Among the 19 correlation indexes illustrated in Table 1.1, there are eight special cases of Pearson's r and two estimates of Pearson's r. Pearson's r is probably the most widely used statistic when describing the relationship between variables. It has been estimated that Pearson's r and its special cases are chosen 95% of the time in research to describe a relationship or to infer a population correlation, ρ (Glass & Hopkins, 1996). Because of its importance and popularity, we will devote Chapters 2, 3, 4, and 5 to various topics pertaining to Pearson's r. Specifically, we will discuss the conceptual meaning of Pearson's r, assumptions, and six different null hypothesis tests in Chapter 2. After that, we will introduce eight special cases of Pearson's r: the phi coefficient (ϕ), the eta coefficient (η), the Spearman rank-order correlation (r_{rank}), the point-biserial correlation (r_{pb}), and four less known correlation indexes (r_{MD}, r_{DR}, r_{MR}, and r_{RI}). We will also present two estimates of Pearson's r, the biserial coefficient (r_{bis}) and the tetrachoric coefficient (r_{tet}), in Chapter 3. In Chapter 4, we will illustrate the other uses of Pearson's r in research and in practice, namely, effect size, power analysis, meta-analysis, utility analysis, reliability estimates, and validation. To prevent potential misinterpretations or misuses of Pearson's r, we will discuss the factors that affect Pearson's r in Chapter 5. In addition, we will introduce the first-order partial correlation ($r_{xy, z}$) as well as two related significance tests in statistical control and model testing. In the final chapter, seven additional nonparametric correlation indexes (contingency coefficient, C, Cramér's V coefficient, Kendall's τ coefficients (τ and τ_b), Stuart's τ_c coefficient, Goodman and Kruskal's γ coefficient, and Kendall's partial rank-order correlation, $\tau_{XY, Z}$) will be presented.

2. THE PEARSON PRODUCT-MOMENT CORRELATION

Pearson's r is called the "product-moment correlation" because it is calculated by multiplying the z scores of two variables (i.e., the product of two variables) and then calculating the average (i.e., the moment) of these products based on a group of n cases. Specifically, variables X and Y are first assessed for n cases. After that, the standardized scores, z_{X_i} and z_{Y_i}, for case i are converted from the correspondent raw scores, X_i and Y_i, based on the linear transformation equation

$$z_{X_i} = \frac{X_i - \overline{X}}{s_X} \quad \text{and} \quad z_{Y_i} = \frac{Y_i - \overline{Y}}{s_Y},$$

where $\overline{X}$ and $\overline{Y}$ are the means of variables X and Y and

$$s_X = \sqrt{\frac{\sum (X_i - \overline{X})^2}{n}} \quad \text{and} \quad s_Y = \sqrt{\frac{\sum (Y_i - \overline{Y})^2}{n}}$$

are the standard deviations of X and Y, respectively. Finally, Pearson's r is calculated by the equation of $(\sum z_{X_i} z_{Y_i})/n$, which is an average of $\sum z_{X_i} z_{Y_i}$ (Cohen & Cohen, 1983). Using the values for z_{X_i} and z_{Y_i} as described in Table 2.1, $\sum z_{X_i} z_{Y_i} = 5.43284$. Therefore, the average product of variables X and Y, Pearson's r, is 0.22. The range of Pearson's r must fall between -1 and 1, and it treats both variables symmetrically. Specifically, Pearson's r of X and Y is the same as that of Y and X.

It should be stressed that the size of Pearson's r in absolute value is not affected by any linear transformation of X or Y. Suppose $A_i = eX_i + f$ and $B_i = gY_i + h$ (e, f, g, and h are constants, and neither e nor g is 0). It can be mathematically proved that $|z_{X_i}| = |z_{A_i}|$ and $|z_{Y_i}| = |z_{B_i}|$. Therefore,

$$\left| \frac{\sum z_{X_i} z_{Y_i}}{n} \right| = \left| \frac{\sum z_{A_i} z_{B_i}}{n} \right| = |r|.$$

Conceptually, z_{X_i} and z_{Y_i} reflect the relative standing of each case i to all of the n cases on variables X and Y, because z_{X_i} and z_{Y_i} are primarily determined by $(X_i - \overline{X})$ and $(Y_i - \overline{Y})$, respectively. If a person i scores high on both variables, the product of $(X_i - \overline{X})$ and $(Y_i - \overline{Y})$ is large and positive. Similarly, if this person scores relatively low on both variables, he or she will have relatively large negative z scores on both variables and the product of $(X_i - \overline{X})$ and $(Y_i - \overline{Y})$ is also large and positive. If the average sum of products of $(X_i - \overline{X})$ and $(Y_i - \overline{Y})$ is positive, a positive relationship between X and Y occurs. Conversely, if the average sum of the products of $(X_i - \overline{X})$ and $(Y_i - \overline{Y})$ is negative, X would be negatively related to Y. For instance, a negative relationship may appear when high (positive)

TABLE 2.1
Computation Components in the Pearson
Product-Moment Correlation

X	Y	XY	X^2	Y^2	$z_x z_y$
18	12	216	324	144	0.6717
14	8	112	196	64	−0.1185
12	6	72	144	36	0.10372
6	4	24	36	16	1.88997
19	4	76	361	16	−1.8554
12	5	60	144	25	0.13253
8	8	64	64	64	0.37536
18	4	72	324	16	−1.5673
19	6	114	361	36	−1.1928
14	10	140	196	100	0.02963
16	18	288	256	324	1.48662
12	16	192	144	256	−0.1844
18	19	342	324	361	2.63081
16	16	256	256	256	1.13266
10	12	120	100	144	−0.3161
8	8	64	64	64	0.37536
6	6	36	36	36	1.21498
4	10	40	16	100	−0.1762
14	6	84	196	36	−0.2667
12	16	192	144	256	−0.1844
10	12	120	100	144	−0.3161
12	8	96	144	64	0.0461
8	8	64	64	64	0.37536
10	6	60	100	36	0.47414
18	12	216	324	144	0.6717

$\sum X_i = 314$ $\quad \sum Y_i = 240$ $\quad \sum X_i Y_i = 3120$ $\quad \sum X_i^2 = 4418$ $\quad \sum Y_i^2 = 2802$ $\quad \sum z_{X_i} z_{Y_i} = 5.43284$

$s_X = 4.355$ $\quad s_Y = 4.463$

z scores of one variable are associated with low (negative) z scores on the other variable in some cases, while the reverse may be found in other cases.

A computation formula for Pearson's r, derived from $(\sum z_{X_i} z_{Y_i})/n$, is demonstrated as

$$\frac{\sum \frac{(X_i - \bar{X})(Y_i - \bar{Y})}{n}}{s_X s_Y} \quad \text{or} \quad \frac{\sum X_i Y_i - \frac{\sum X_i \sum Y_i}{n}}{\sqrt{\left(\sum X_i^2 - \frac{(\sum X_i)^2}{n}\right)\left(\sum Y_i^2 - \frac{(\sum Y_i)^2}{n}\right)}}.$$

The numerator of the first equation refers to the covariance, which represents an average of the sum of covariation between X and Y and reflects relationships between X and Y. Covariance can be either a positive or a negative value, and that determines the direction of Pearson's r. However, its value changes contingent upon the different measurement units employed by X and Y, which can make the covariance of X and Y difficult to interpret. If we standardize the covariance of X and Y, $(\sum(X_i - \overline{X})(Y_i - \overline{Y}))/n$, by dividing by the correspondent standard deviations s_X and s_Y, it can be shown that

$$\sum \frac{(X_i - \overline{X})(Y_i - \overline{Y})}{s_X s_Y n} = \frac{\sum\left[\left(\frac{(X_i - \overline{X})}{s_X}\right)\left(\frac{(Y_i - \overline{Y})}{s_Y}\right)\right]}{n}.$$

This equation is actually the same as $(\sum z_{X_i} z_{Y_i})/n$. In sum, Pearson's r can also be viewed as a standardized covariance. Substituting the data provided in the last row of Table 2.1, Pearson's r equals 0.22. Calculation of Pearson's r is available in almost all statistical packages, as well as in many database programs (e.g., Excel®).

Interpretation of Pearson's *r*

Practically, Pearson's r is viewed as an indicator that describes a linear interdependence between variables X and Y, with the form of $Y = a + (b) \times X$, where a and b are constants. In general, the larger the magnitude (in absolute value), the more interdependence between the variables. When X and Y are *not* interdependent (i.e., they are independent), this implies that the population correlation coefficient (ρ) is 0. However, the existence of $\rho = 0$ does not necessarily indicate the independence of X and Y *unless* the bivariate normal distribution assumption (discussed below) holds. For instance, a curvilinear relationship between X and Y (a topic in Chapter 5) suggests that both variables are interdependent, even though Pearson's r might be 0.

Furthermore, Pearson's r does not refer to a proportion, nor does it represent the proportionate strength of a relationship. For example, a correlation of 0.6 is not twice the relationship of a correlation of 0.3. In contrast to Pearson's r, the value of r^2 (also referred to as the coefficient of determination) can be interpreted as a proportion. Suppose the correlation coefficient of stock price and corporate profit of a Fortune 500 company is 0.6. The r^2 value of 0.36 is interpreted as 36% of the variance in stock price shared, explained, predicted, or accounted for by corporate profit or vice versa, and this is twice the variance explained had the r^2 value been 0.18.

Assumptions of Pearson's r in Inferential Statistics

Pearson's r can be used as a descriptive statistic, similar to the mean, mode, or standard deviation. When Pearson's r is calculated to describe characteristics of a sample, it does not require any assumptions. However, if researchers attempt to use a sample Pearson's r to infer the population, ρ, or to conduct null hypothesis tests, a bivariate normal distribution is generally assumed. Both variables X and Y follow a bivariate normal distribution if and only if, for every possible linear combination W, $W = c_1 X + c_2 Y$, the distribution of W is normal with neither c values being 0 (Hays, 1994). An example of a bivariate normal distribution when $\rho = 0$ is depicted in Figure 2.1.

In a bivariate normal distribution, the relationship between X and Y cannot be described by anything *but* a linear function (Hays, 1994). In addition, both marginal distributions of X and Y are normal (marginal distributions of X and Y being merely the distributions of

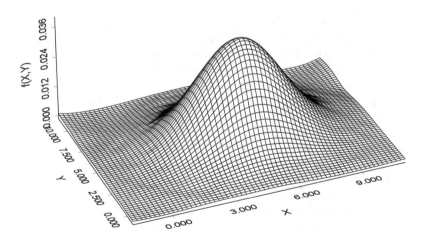

Figure 2.1. Bivariate Normal Distribution of X and Y When $\rho_{xy} = 0$, $\sigma_x = \sigma_y = 2$, $\mu_x = \mu_y = 5$

X and Y). Furthermore, at each value of X (or Y), there is a normal distribution of Y (or X). These distributions are referred to as the conditional distributions of Y (or X). It should be noted that normal marginal distributions of X and Y do not necessarily mean that the bivariate distribution is normal. It is possible to have a nonlinear relationship between X and Y when both marginal distributions are normal.

Sampling Distributions of Pearson's r

A clear understanding of the concept of sampling distribution is paramount for researchers when computing inferential statistics based on sample statistics, such as using a sample r to infer ρ, the population correlation. Before we present a series of inferential statistics in the remaining sections, we will first introduce the concept of sampling distribution.

A sampling distribution is a theoretical probability distribution that describes the functional relationship between *all* possible values of a given statistic (e.g., r) based on a sample of n cases and the probability associated with each value. Assume that there exists a population of N pairs of (X, Y) and the population correlation, ρ, between X and Y is equal to 0. Suppose we randomly select the first n pairs of (X_n, Y_n) from the population, calculate Pearson's r based on the first sample, and put this set of (X_n, Y_n) back into the population. Imagine that we repeatedly follow the above procedure and obtain all possible samples of n pairs of (X_n, Y_n) from the population. All possible values of Pearson's r based on the sample size of n, and the probabilities of observing each value of Pearson's r, can be obtained accordingly. Finally, we can construct a sampling distribution of Pearson's r, given $\rho = 0$, that illustrates the functional relationship between the values of Pearson's r shown on the X axis and the correspondent probability shown on the Y axis.

Using this distribution, we will be able to find the correspondent probability if a particular sample Pearson's r is known. Intuitively, we know that there is a small chance that we could obtain a large-sample Pearson's r when $\rho = 0$. Conversely, there is a large probability that we could obtain a small-sample Pearson's r when $\rho = 0$. Because each sampling distribution of Pearson's r varies contingent upon the value of ρ and the sample size of n, there are infinite sampling distributions of Pearson's r. If all the sampling distributions of Pearson's r share common properties, it would be very easy for us to make statements about how likely it would be to observe a sample r, given a sample size of n and a population of ρ.

Properties of the Sampling Distribution of Pearson's r

There are a few important characteristics that are shared by all the sampling distributions of Pearson's r. First, the sampling distribution of Pearson's r does not approximate normality for small sample sizes. When n increases, distributions will approximate normal more slowly when $\rho \neq 0$ than when $\rho = 0$. When $\rho \neq 0$ and $|\rho|$ increases, the sampling distributions tend to be skewed with small sample sizes. Specifically, the sampling distribution of Pearson's r becomes negatively skewed (i.e., the tail is skewed to the left) when a nonzero ρ (denoted by $\rho_\varnothing$) is positive. The larger the $\rho_\varnothing$, the more negatively skewed the distribution. Conversely, the distribution is skewed to the right when $\rho_\varnothing$ is negative. The more negative the $\rho_\varnothing$, the more positively skewed the distribution.

To eliminate the skewness of sampling distributions of Pearson's r when $|\rho_\varnothing|$ increases, Fisher (1921) suggests transforming values of r into a new variable z_r based on

$$z_r = 0.5 \times \log_e \left(\frac{1+r}{1-r} \right),$$

where $\log_e$ is the natural logarithm function. After the transformation, the sampling distributions of z_r (rather than Pearson's r) become asymptotically normal. That is, the distributions approach normality with an increase in sample size. This normality feature is very appealing in null hypothesis testing. The difference between Pearson's r and Fisher's z_r is negligible when Pearson's r is around or below 0.3 in absolute value. However, the difference becomes noticeable when Pearson's r increases beyond this range.

Second, when $\rho = 0$ or $\rho = 1$, the mean of the sampling distribution of Pearson's r is equal to 0 or 1, respectively. Putting it differently, $E(r) = \rho$ when $\rho = 0$ or $\rho = 1$. Note that $E(r)$ is the expected value of all possible values of Pearson's r in a sampling distribution, which can be viewed as the average of all possible values of Pearson's r. Because $E(r) = \rho$ when $\rho = 0$ or $\rho = 1$, a sample Pearson's r is considered to be an unbiased estimator of the population correlation in the long run. That is, compared to other sample statistics, a sample Pearson's r is the best estimator to indicate the population correlation ρ when $\rho = 0$ or 1.

When either $\rho \neq 0$ or $\rho \neq 1$, however, Pearson's r is a biased estimator of ρ, although the bias is generally small. The relatively unbiased estimator of $|\rho|$ is $\{[(n-1)r^2 - 1]/(n-2)\}^{1/2}$, which is smaller than $|r|$. The phenomenon of $E(\{[(n-1)r^2 - 1]/(n-2)\}^{1/2})$ being smaller than $|r|$ refers to shrinkage, which results from the fallible (or sampling-error prone) means and standard deviations of a sample (Wherry, 1984). Note that the transformed value of a population ρ (either $\rho \neq 0$ or $\rho \neq 1$) is the same as the mean of a sampling distribution of z_r. That is,

$$\mathrm{E}(z_r) = z_\rho \quad \text{or} \quad 0.5 \times \log_e\left(\frac{1+\rho}{1-\rho}\right).$$

Third, the standard error (i.e., standard deviation) of the sampling distribution of Pearson's r based on large n samples is approximately $[(1-\rho^2)^2/n]^{1/2}$, and the standard error of the sampling distribution of z_r is approximately $[1/(n-3)]^{1/2}$.

Null Hypothesis Tests of $\rho = 0$

Based on a sample Pearson's r, researchers may be interested in examining if its population correlation coefficient, ρ, is different from 0. The null hypothesis is $\rho = 0$, and the alternative hypothesis can be $\rho > 0, \rho < 0$, or $\rho \neq 0$. The former two alternative hypotheses are directional hypotheses, and the one-tailed test would be used in hypothesis testing. In contrast, the last hypothesis is nondirectional, and the two-tailed test would be used in this hypothesis-testing situation. Conventionally, researchers determine a probability of α (e.g., 0.05 or 0.01) in advance as a standard or significance level. Based on the correspondent sampling distribution, we would reject the null hypothesis if the probability that we would observe a sample correlation were smaller than α.

When $\rho = 0$, the sampling distribution of the statistic $\frac{r\sqrt{n-2}}{\sqrt{1-r^2}}$ is distributed as a t distribution, which varies contingent upon the degrees of freedom (denoted by df), $n-2$. That is, $t = \frac{r\sqrt{n-2}}{\sqrt{1-r^2}}$ when $\rho = 0$. Suppose a correlation between satisfaction with a ski resort and number of lift chairs operating in a ski resort (based on a sample of 102 skiers) is 0.3. To test the hypothesis that ρ is different from 0, the null hypothesis (H_0) is stated as $\rho = 0$, the alternative hypothesis (H_1) is stated as $\rho \neq 0$, and the significance level or the probability of α is set as 0.05. Based on the above formula, we obtain $t = 3.14$. The observed t value is greater than the critical t value, 1.98 (refer to Appendix 1), which suggests that there is a small chance (less than 0.05) that we would obtain a t value of 3.14 in a t sampling distribution, with a df of 100. In other words, it is quite unlikely that we would observe a correlation of 0.3 in the above sampling distribution when $\rho = 0$ with a df of 100. Therefore, we reject the null hypothesis and conclude that 0.3 is significantly different from $\rho = 0$.

If we are interested in examining if ρ is greater than 0, the alternative hypothesis (H_1) in the above example would be changed to $\rho > 0$. Following the same procedure, the observed t value is greater than the critical t value of 1.66, $\alpha = 0.05$, or the critical value of 2.36, $\alpha = 0.01$ (see Appendix 1). Accordingly, we would reject the null hypothesis and conclude that 0.3 is significantly greater than the population correlation, $\rho = 0$.

Results of the null hypothesis test of $\rho = 0$ are routinely reported throughout the scientific literature, and these results are typically presented in a correlation matrix format, which is the default output generated by most, if not all, statistical programs. However, it is important to recognize potential problems when interpreting the correlation matrix.

For example, the correlation matrix depicted in Table 2.2 describes 21 Pearson's rs (reported in the first row within each cell) among seven patient satisfaction measures, in conjunction with 21 null hypothesis tests of $\rho = 0$ (reported in the second row within each cell) reported by SPSS®. The number of intercorrelations among k variables can be quickly calculated by $[k(k-1)]/2$. Imagine the number of studied variables increases twofold or threefold, resulting in 91 or 210 Pearson's rs (respectively) reported in a correlation matrix. Compared to the increase in the number of studied variables, the number of intercorrelations increases more rapidly, in conjunction with the same number of null hypothesis tests of $\rho = 0$. It should be emphasized here (although it is often neglected or overlooked in practice) that a large volume of null hypothesis tests of $\rho = 0$ presented in a correlation matrix leads to a high probability of committing a Type I error (i.e., rejection of the null hypothesis when the null hypothesis is true).

TABLE 2.2
Example of a Correlation Matrix

Correlations

		Satisfaction With Physicians	Satisfaction With Nursing Aids	Satisfaction With Nurses	Satisfaction With Receptionists	Satisfaction With Physical Therapists	Satisfaction With Respiratory Therapists	Satisfaction With Physician Assistants
Satisfaction with physicians	Pearson correlation	1.00						
	Sig. (2-tailed)							
	N							
Satisfaction with nursing aids	Pearson correlation	.290	1.00					
	Sig. (2-tailed)	.002						
	N	107						
Satisfaction with nurses	Pearson correlation	.128	.360	1.00				
	Sig. (2-tailed)	.186	.000					
	N	109	107					
Satisfaction with receptionists	Pearson correlation	.021	.497	.627	1.00			
	Sig. (2-tailed)	.825	.000	.000				
	N	109	107	109				
Satisfaction with physical therapists	Pearson correlation	.146	.197	.481	.357	1.00		
	Sig. (2-tailed)	.128	.042	.000	.000			
	N	110	107	109	109			
Satisfaction with respiratory therapists	Pearson correlation	.269	.138	.066	.080	.272	1.00	
	Sig. (2-tailed)	.005	.161	.498	.417	.005		
	N	107	105	106	106	107		
Satisfaction with physician assistants	Pearson correlation	.304	.122	.344	.167	.422	.212	1.00
	Sig. (2-tailed)	.001	.215	.000	.085	.000	.030	
	N	107	105	107	107	107	105	

Null Hypothesis Tests of $\rho = \rho_\varnothing$

Compared to the null hypothesis test of $\rho = 0$, it is probably more interesting and informative, both in practice and in research, to examine the null hypothesis of $\rho = \rho_\varnothing$, where $\rho_\varnothing$ is a nonzero population correlation coefficient. Suppose a testing company develops a quantitative aptitude test (referred to as the V test) and plans to market this test to be used in graduate school admissions. A VP in the marketing department raises the following question: "How much does the V test outperform its competitor, the Graduate Record Examination (GRE) verbal test [referred to as the GREV], in predicting the first-year graduate grade point average (GPA)?" Suppose the estimated population correlation of GREV and the first-year graduate GPA is 0.32, and that is chosen to be the comparison standard. If the V test has shown a relationship of 0.50 with the first-year graduate GPA based on a group of 53 first-year graduate students, the VP's question can be rephrased as "Is the correlation of 0.50 stronger than the standard of 0.32?"

To answer questions similar to those posed above, we can conduct a null hypothesis test of $\rho = \rho_\varnothing$. According to the question, H_0: $\rho = \rho_\varnothing = 0.32$ and H_1: $\rho > \rho_\varnothing$. Recall that sampling distributions of Pearson's r become highly skewed when $|\rho|$ increases. In contrast, the sampling distributions of Fisher's z_r are approximately normal. Therefore, we can easily conduct the null hypothesis test by using the formula

$$z = \frac{z_r - z_\varnothing}{\sqrt{1/(n-3)}},$$

where z_r is the transformed value of Pearson's r of a sample (i.e., 0.5 in this example) and $z_\varnothing$ is the transformed value of $\rho_\varnothing$ (i.e., 0.32). The value of the z statistic describes how many units of standard error z_r is from $z_\varnothing$, given that the null hypothesis is true. According to the above formula, we find $z_r = 0.54931$, $z_\varnothing = 0.33165$, and $z = 1.54$. Based on αs of 0.05 and 0.01, the critical z values in the absolute value are approximately 1.65 and 2.33 for a one-tailed test (1.96 and 2.58 for a two-tailed test). Therefore, we fail to reject the null hypothesis. Putting it more practically, the predictability of the V test does not significantly outperform that of the GREV.

In general, the above inferential tests tend not to inflate the Type I error when the normality assumption is violated, as long as n

approaches 20 or 30, and each pair of (X, Y) is measured independently from other pairs (Edgell & Noon, 1984). If pairs of (X, Y) are not independent from each other, the Type I error is severely inflated, even when n approaches 100.

Confidence Intervals of ρ

Although a population ρ can be estimated by a point such as a sample r or $\{[(n-1)r^2 - 1]/(n-2)\}^{1/2}$ (the unbiased estimator of $|\rho|$ when $\rho \neq 0$ or $\rho \neq 1$), it can also be estimated by an interval between two points, referred to as a confidence interval. Given a sample size of n and a sample r, the approximate 95% confidence interval is

$$z_r - 1.96\sqrt{\frac{1}{n-3}} \leq z_\rho \leq z_r + 1.96\sqrt{\frac{1}{n-3}},$$

and the 99% confidence interval is

$$z_r - 2.58\sqrt{\frac{1}{n-3}} \leq z_\rho \leq z_r + 2.58\sqrt{\frac{1}{n-3}},$$

where z_ρ is the transformed value of ρ.

Substituting a sample Pearson's r of 0.5 ($z_r = 0.549306$) based on 103 subjects, the 95% confidence interval for z_ρ is estimated to be $0.35 \leq z_\rho \leq 0.75$. Since 0.35, 0.75, and z_ρ are the transformed values, we need to find the corresponding correlations, which can be obtained by

$$r = \frac{e^{2z_r} - 1}{e^{2z_r} + 1}.$$

Converting z_r back to r, the 95% confidence interval for ρ is $0.34 \leq \rho \leq 0.64$.

Null Hypothesis Test of $\rho_1 = \rho_2$

Both in practice and in research, we often encounter problems such as whether a correlation in sample A (ρ_1) is different from the very same correlation in sample B (ρ_2). In these cases, it is important not to confuse the null hypothesis test of $\rho_1 = \rho_2$ with the null hypothesis test of $\rho = \rho_\varnothing$. In contrast to the null hypothesis test of $\rho = \rho_\varnothing$, the former is an inferential statistical test for the difference between two correlations calculated from two *independent* samples A and B. The latter is an inferential statistical test for the difference between a correlation calculated from a single sample and a specific standard correlation chosen by researchers.

Below is a practical application of the null hypothesis test of $\rho_1 = \rho_2$. A human resources manager plans to use a personnel selection test that is presumably nondiscriminatory in predicting job performance. Before this manager officially uses the test to select both male and female employees, he or she examines if the correlations between test score and job performance differ between male and female employees. If the correlations differ between male and female employees, it suggests that the test may suffer from discriminatory problems.

To examine if the correlation in sample A differs from that in sample B, we can conduct a z test according to the formula

$$z = \frac{z_{r_1} - z_{r_2}}{\sqrt{1/(n_1 - 3) + 1/(n_2 - 3)}},$$

where both z_{r_1} and z_{r_2} are transformed Fisher's z_r values of Pearson's r of sample A and sample B, respectively, and n_1 and n_2 are sample sizes of sample A and sample B, respectively. The correlation based on 103 female employees in the above example is 0.3, and the correlation of 103 male employees is 0.55. H_0 is stated as $\rho_1 = \rho_2$, and H_1 is stated as $\rho_1 \neq \rho_2$. We first transform the two Pearson's rs into Fisher's z_rs and substitute the corresponding values into the above formula. We obtain $z = 2.18$, which is greater than the critical value of 1.96 if α is determined as 0.05, but is smaller than the critical value of 2.58 if α is set as 0.01. Based on the standard of 0.05, the human resources manager would reject the null hypothesis and conclude that the correlation in the male group differs from that in the female group. However, the manager would fail to reject the null hypothesis should α be 0.01.

In addition to the above two-tailed test, the one-tailed test for the difference between two correlations is often employed. For instance, social support has been proposed to be a buffering factor that serves as a cushion when people face stressful circumstances. Specifically, people will experience less strain when facing stressful incidents (e.g., job loss or terminal disease) if they receive strong emotional support from members of their social network. Therefore, it is reasonable to hypothesize that the relationship between stressful incidents and strain is weaker among people who receive strong social support than among those receiving little social support. Suppose the correlations between stressor and strain are 0.15 for 103 people who are receiving strong social support and 0.4 for 103 people who are receiving low social support. Accordingly, H_0 is stated as $\rho_1 = \rho_2$, H_1 is stated as $\rho_1 < \rho_2$, and $z = 1.93$. The observed z value is greater than the critical value of 1.65 ($\alpha = 0.05$) and supports the buffering hypothesis. In contrast, the observed value is smaller than the critical value of 2.33 ($\alpha = 0.01$), which fails to support the hypothesis under more stringent requirements.

Null Hypothesis Test for the Difference Among More Than Two Independent ρs

The above hypothesis test is applicable only when examining the difference in correlations between two independent samples. In more practical contexts, we often need to investigate the difference in correlations among more than two independent samples. For example, an educational policymaker wants to find out if the correlation between Scholastic Aptitude Test (SAT) and college GPA differs among school districts. The correlation and sample size of each district are presented in Table 2.3. To examine if these 10 correlations are different from one another, he or she can conduct a χ^2 test of homogeneity:

$$\chi^2 = \sum(n_k - 3)z_{r_k}^2 - \frac{[\sum(n_k - 3)z_{r_k}]^2}{\sum(n_k - 3)}, \qquad df = k - 1, \ k > 1,$$

where n_k refers to the sample size in sample k and z_{r_k} refers to the transformed Fisher's z_r value of Pearson's r of sample k. The null hypothesis is stated as $\rho_1 = \rho_2 = \cdots = \rho_k = \rho$, and the alternative hypothesis is stated as "at least one correlation is different from ρ."

Substituting the data of the last row in Table 2.3 into the above formula, we obtain an observed χ^2 value of 66.32, with a df of 9:

$$\chi^2 = 954.50 - \frac{(1587.1)^2}{2836} = 66.32, \qquad df = 9.$$

TABLE 2.3
Correlations Between SAT and College GPA
Among 10 School Districts

District k	r	n_k	z_{r_k}	$n_k - 3$	$z_{r_k}^2$	$(n_k - 3) z_{r_k}^2$	$(n_k - 3) z_{r_k}$
1	0.70	165	0.8673	162	0.75221	121.858	140.503
2	0.46	293	0.49731	290	0.24732	71.7224	144.22
3	0.57	302	0.64752	299	0.41929	125.366	193.609
4	0.50	398	0.54931	395	0.30174	119.186	216.976
5	0.32	482	0.33165	479	0.10999	52.6851	158.859
6	0.45	329	0.4847	326	0.23493	76.5886	158.012
7	0.70	191	0.8673	188	0.75221	141.416	163.052
8	0.49	137	0.53606	134	0.28736	38.5063	71.8321
9	0.58	275	0.66246	272	0.43886	119.369	180.19
10	0.50	294	0.54931	291	0.30174	87.8055	159.848
Σ				2836		954.5033	1587.102

According to the χ^2 table presented in Appendix 2, the observed χ^2 value is greater than the critical value of 16.92 ($\alpha = 0.05$) or 21.67 ($\alpha = 0.01$), which suggests that the correlation between SAT score and GPA does differ among the school districts. Before we move to the next section, it should be noted that the null hypothesis test of $\rho_1 = \rho_2$ is just a special case of the χ^2 test for homogeneity. Essentially, both tests will reach the same results because the squared z value is the same as the χ^2 value with a df of 1.

Null Hypothesis Test for the Difference
Between Two Dependent Correlations

Sometimes, we are faced with situations in which the correlations are not independent. Suppose four variables, J, K, H, and M, are measured for a group of subjects. The correlations between J and K, J and H, J and M, K and H, as well as H and M are not, in general, independent of each other (Steiger, 1980). As a result, the independent test of $\rho_1 = \rho_2$ is no longer appropriate. Compared to the previous inferential tests, the null hypothesis test for the equality of two dependent correlations is probably less often applied, although it can be very useful. Below are two scenarios, which require two different null hypothesis tests.

Case 1.   Is a variable J related to a variable K differently than to a variable H? For example, a physician is interested in finding out if the frequency of use of a drug (variable J) is more related to weight gain (variable K) than related to hair loss (variable H) based on 103 patients. The null hypothesis is stated as $\rho_{jk} = \rho_{jh}$, and the alternative hypothesis is $\rho_{jk} > \rho_{jh}$.

Case 2.   Is the relationship between variable J and variable K different from that between variable H and variable M? For example, a political consultant is interested in finding out from a sample of voters if the relationship between party donations (variable J) and intention to vote (variable K) four years ago is different from the relationship between party donations (variable H) and intention to vote (variable M) this year. The null hypothesis is stated as $\rho_{jk} = \rho_{hm}$, and the alternative hypothesis is $\rho_{jk} \neq \rho_{hm}$.

To examine the null hypothesis described in Case 1, Steiger (1980) suggested that Williams's t test can be used with confidence when the sample size exceeds 20. The t-test formula is

$$t = (r_{jk} - r_{jh})\sqrt{\frac{(n-1)(1+r_{kh})}{2((n-1)/(n-3))|R| + \bar{r}^2(1-r_{kh})^3}}, \quad df = n-3,$$

where $|R| = 1 - r_{jk}^2 - r_{jh}^2 - r_{kh}^2 + 2r_{jk}r_{jh}r_{kh}$ and $\bar{r} = (r_{jk} + r_{jh})/2$. Following the example for Case 1, suppose the correlation between frequency of drug use (J) and weight gain (K), r_{jk}, is 0.5, the correlation between frequency of drug use (J) and hair loss (H), r_{jh}, is 0.2, and the correlation between weight gain (K) and hair loss (H), r_{kh}, is 0.3. Substituting the above data into the formula, we obtain $|R| = 0.68$, $\bar{r} = 0.35$, and $t = 2.89$. The observed t value is greater than the critical t value of 1.66 if α is 0.05 or 2.36 if α is 0.01, which suggests that the frequency of drug use is more strongly related to weight gain than to hair loss.

Regarding the null hypothesis for Case 2, Steiger (1980) suggested the use of Dunn and Clark's z test if n exceeds 20. That is,

$$z = (z_{r_{jk}} - z_{r_{hm}})\sqrt{\frac{n-3}{2-2\bar{s}}}, \quad \bar{s} = \frac{\psi}{(1-\bar{r}^2)^2}, \quad \bar{r} = \frac{r_{jk} + r_{hm}}{2},$$

where $z_{r_{jk}}$ and $z_{r_{hm}}$ are transformed Fisher's z_r values of Pearson's r_{jk} and r_{hm} and

$$\psi = 0.5\{[(r_{jh} - r_{kh}\bar{r})(r_{km} - r_{kh}\bar{r})] + [(r_{jm} - r_{jh}\bar{r})(r_{kh} - r_{jh}\bar{r})]$$
$$+ [(r_{jh} - r_{jm}\bar{r})(r_{km} - r_{jm}\bar{r})] + [(r_{jm} - r_{km}\bar{r})(r_{kh} - r_{km}\bar{r})]\}.$$

Based on the example in Case 2, suppose $r_{jk} = 0.3$, $r_{hm} = 0.4$, $r_{jh} = 0.6$, $r_{jm} = 0.2$, $r_{kh} = 0.3$, $r_{km} = 0.7$, and $n = 203$. Substituting the data into the above equations, $\bar{r} = 0.35$, $\psi = 0.3125$, $\bar{s} = 0.4059$, and $z = -1.48$. According to the result, the political consultant fails to reject the null hypothesis of $\rho_{jk} = \rho_{hm}$ and concludes that there is not sufficient evidence to show that the relationship between party donations and intention to vote fluctuates across two different times.

Null hypothesis tests of equality among dependent correlations have not received much attention in the scientific literature or in the practice world. To the best of our knowledge, these statistical tests are not available in any major statistical program packages. Nonetheless, there are many useful and practical applications. It is also useful to know that the null hypothesis tests described here can usually be used with the variations of Pearson's r statistic that are presented next in Chapter 3.

3. SPECIAL CASES OF PEARSON'S r

In this chapter, we will introduce three widely used indexes of relationships: the point-biserial correlation (r_{pb}), the phi coefficient (ϕ), and the Spearman rank-order correlation (r_{rank}). Because these correlations are special cases of Pearson's r (Cohen & Cohen, 1983), all the null hypothesis tests previously described in Chapter 2 are generally applicable. In addition, the correspondent computational equations demonstrated in this chapter are mainly mathematically simplified versions of Pearson's r formula. Note that the absolute value of these correlations tends to be smaller than 1, because the shapes of the distributions of X and Y are often not symmetrical or do not have the same forms (a topic to be elaborated on in Chapter 5).

Following the presentation of these three indexes, we will discuss two less often used indexes: the biserial coefficient (r_{bis}) and the tetrachoric coefficient (r_{tet}), which are estimates of the point-biserial correlation and phi coefficient, respectively. At the end of this chapter, we will introduce the eta coefficient (η), which gauges the association between a multichotomous variable (e.g., race) and a continuous variable. In addition, we will briefly discuss four special cases of Pearson's r that are less well known to researchers: r_{MD}, r_{DR}, r_{MR}, and r_{RI} (Wherry, 1984).

Point-Biserial Correlation, r_{pb}

When Pearson's r is applied to assess the relationship between a true dichotomous variable X (e.g., gender) and a continuous variable Y (e.g., age), this correlation refers to the point-biserial correlation (r_{pb}). Essentially, inference of r_{pb} provides the same information as that of an independent two-sample t test, although they have a different focus. The former stresses the existence of a relationship, and the latter focuses on the difference between two means. The independent two-sample t test is probably one of the most well known statistics, introduced in all elementary statistics textbooks. However, its relationship with the point-biserial correlation is often either overlooked or misinterpreted.

Let us start with an example of an independent two-sample t test to introduce the meaning of r_{pb}. Suppose a political scientist is interested in gender differences (denoted by X) in candidate liking (denoted by Y). The researcher surveys 20 male and 20 female registered voters. Each respondent rates how much he or she likes a candidate on a 10-point scale. The higher the scores, the stronger the liking. The findings are reproduced in Table 3.1. According to the independent two-sample t test based on

$$t = (\overline{Y}_1 - \overline{Y}_2) \Big/ \sqrt{\frac{s_P^2}{n_1} + \frac{s_P^2}{n_2}}, \qquad df = (n_1 + n_2 - 2),$$

$$s_P^2 = \frac{(n_1 - 1)s_1^2 + (n_2 - 1)s_2^2}{(n_1 - 1) + (n_2 - 1)},$$

where s_1^2 and s_2^2 are the estimated variances ($\sum(Y - \overline{Y})^2/(n-1)$) of the population of Y for samples 1 and 2, $\overline{Y}_1$ and $\overline{Y}_2$ are the means on Y for samples 1 and 2, and n_1 and n_2 are the sizes of samples 1 and 2. Substituting the data in Table 3.1, $s_P^2 = 4.36$, and $t = 3.10$, $p < 0.05$, two-tailed, which suggests there is a significant mean difference on

TABLE 3.1

Result of an Independent Two-Sample t Test:
Candidate Liking Between Male and Female Voters

Male		Female	
8	10	2	8
6	4	6	1
8	8	6	6
10	10	8	8
8	8	7	6
6	10	2	5
4	8	3	4
9	6	10	4
6	6	4	6
7	7	6	6

$\overline{Y}_1 = 7.45,\ s_1^2 = 3.418,\ n_1 = 20 \qquad \overline{Y}_2 = 5.4,\ s_2^2 = 5.305,\ n_2 = 20$

$$s_P^2 = \frac{(20-1) \times 3.418 + (20-1) \times 5.305}{(20-1) + (20-1)} = 4.36,$$

$t(38) = 3.10,\ p < 0.05$, two-tailed

candidate liking between males and females. Specifically, female voters like the candidate less than do male voters.

Using the above data, we can also calculate the point-biserial correlation between gender (X) and candidate liking (Y) by means of Pearson's r formula, if the data are rearranged as shown in Table 3.2. When male is coded as 1 and female is coded as 2, the correlation coefficient is -0.45. When male is coded as 1 and female is coded as 0, the correlation coefficient becomes 0.45. As pointed out in Chapter 2, the absolute value of a correlation coefficient is not affected by a linear transformation. Because the dichotomous variable X does not share the same marginal distribution as the continuous variable Y, the maximum r_{pb} will always be less than 1.

It should also be noted that the two numerical values chosen for the above coding are arbitrary, and the only requirement is that they be different. The correlation coefficient of -0.45 suggests that the higher the "gender" (i.e., from 1 to 2), the weaker the liking. In other words, female voters (coded as 2) like the candidate less than do male voters (coded as 1). Similarly, the correlation coefficient of $+0.45$ indicates that the higher the "gender" (from 0 to 1), the stronger

TABLE 3.2
Result of the Point-Biserial Correlation
Between Candidate Liking (Y) and Gender (X)

\multicolumn{8}{c}{X (Male = 1 and Female = 2)}								\multicolumn{8}{c}{X (Male = 1 and Female = 0)}							
X	Y	X	Y	X	Y	X	Y	X	Y	X	Y	X	Y	X	Y
2	2	2	8	1	8	1	10	0	2	0	8	1	8	1	10
2	6	2	1	1	6	1	4	0	6	0	1	1	6	1	4
2	6	2	6	1	8	1	8	0	6	0	6	1	8	1	8
2	8	2	8	1	10	1	10	0	8	0	8	1	10	1	10
2	7	2	6	1	8	1	8	0	7	0	6	1	8	1	8
2	2	2	5	1	6	1	10	0	2	0	5	1	6	1	10
2	3	2	4	1	4	1	8	0	3	0	4	1	4	1	8
2	10	2	4	1	9	1	6	0	10	0	4	1	9	1	6
2	4	2	6	1	6	1	6	0	4	0	6	1	6	1	6
2	6	2	6	1	7	1	7	0	6	0	6	1	7	1	7

$\sum XY = 365$, $\sum X = 60$, $\sum X^2 = 100$, $\sum Y = 257$, $\sum Y^2 = 1859$

$\sum XY = 149$, $\sum X = 20$, $\sum X^2 = 20$, $\sum Y = 257$, $\sum Y^2 = 1859$

$$r_{pb} = \frac{365 - \frac{60 \times 257}{40}}{\sqrt{100 - \frac{60^2}{40}}\sqrt{1859 - \frac{257^2}{40}}} = -0.45$$

$$r_{pb} = \frac{149 - \frac{20 \times 257}{40}}{\sqrt{20 - \frac{20^2}{40}}\sqrt{1859 - \frac{257^2}{40}}} = 0.45$$

NOTE: Both r_{pb}s are calculated based on the Pearson's r computation formula.

the liking. Putting it differently, male voters (coded as 1) like the candidate more than do female voters (coded as 0). Results of the null hypothesis test of $\rho = 0$, described in Chapter 2, further indicate that either 0.45 or -0.45 is significantly different from 0, with $t(38) = 3.10$, $p < 0.05$, two-tailed.

In summary, except for the rounding error, the t-statistic value derived from the null hypothesis test of $\rho = 0$ is the same as that derived from the null hypothesis test of $\mu_1 = \mu_2$ shown earlier. The relationship between the point-biserial correlation coefficient and the observed t statistic derived from the two-sample t test can be described by either

$$t = \frac{r_{pb}}{\sqrt{1 - r_{pb}^2}} \times \sqrt{n_1 + n_2 - 2} \quad \text{or} \quad r_{pb}^2 = \frac{t^2}{(n_1 + n_2 - 2) + t^2}.$$

Phi Coefficient, ϕ

The phi coefficient (ϕ) is another special case of Pearson's r that is used when both variables are naturally dichotomous. Let us use the following example to illustrate how to calculate ϕ. An equal opportunity officer in a medical school investigates if there is any association between gender (X) and acceptance (Y). According to the application data, there are 30 female applicants and 40 male applicants. Among the female applicants, 10 are accepted, whereas 25 of the male applicants are accepted.

The resulting data are reproduced in Table 3.3, with female coded as 1 and male coded as 0, and with acceptance coded as 1 and rejection coded as 0. As can be seen, there are 10 pairs of $(1, 1)$, 20 pairs of $(1, 0)$, 25 pairs of $(0, 1)$, and 15 pairs of $(0, 0)$. Based on the Pearson's r formula, the correlation (ϕ) between gender and acceptance is -0.29. This negative correlation suggests that the higher the "gender" (from 0 to 1), the lower the "acceptance" (from 1 to 0). In other words, fewer female applicants (coded as 1 in X) are accepted than are male applicants (coded as 0 in X). Based on the null hypoth-

TABLE 3.3

Acceptance to Medical School Among Male and Female Applicants

X	Y	X	Y	X	Y	X	Y	X	Y	X	Y	X	Y
1	1	1	0	1	0	0	1	0	1	0	1	0	0
1	1	1	0	1	0	0	1	0	1	0	1	0	0
1	1	1	0	1	0	0	1	0	1	0	1	0	0
1	1	1	0	1	0	0	1	0	1	0	1	0	0
1	1	1	0	1	0	0	1	0	1	0	1	0	0
1	1	1	0	1	0	0	1	0	1	0	0	0	0
1	1	1	0	1	0	0	1	0	1	0	0	0	0
1	1	1	0	1	0	0	1	0	1	0	0	0	0
1	1	1	0	1	0	0	1	0	1	0	0	0	0
1	1	1	0	1	0	0	1	0	1	0	0	0	0

$$\sum XY = 10, \ \sum X = 30, \ \sum X^2 = 30, \ \sum Y = 35, \ \sum Y^2 = 35$$

$$\phi = \frac{10 - \frac{30 \times 35}{70}}{\sqrt{30 - \frac{30^2}{70}} \sqrt{35 - \frac{35^2}{70}}} = -0.29$$

NOTE: $X = 1$ (female), $X = 0$ (male); $Y = 1$ (accepted), $Y = 0$ (rejected). ϕ is calculated based on the Pearson's r computation formula.

esis test of $\rho = 0$, the officer concludes that there is a significant association between gender and acceptance, with $t(68) = -2.50$, $p < 0.05$, two-tailed.

The null hypothesis test can also be conducted by using the χ^2 test of independence. Because $\chi^2 = n\phi^2$ with $df = 1$, we can obtain the observed χ^2 value of 5.89, which is greater than the critical value of χ^2 (3.84 at $\alpha = 0.05$, two-tailed). This suggests that gender and acceptance are not independent. In other words, there is a significant association between gender and acceptance.

In Chapter 1, we illustrated Dr. Salk's experiment pertaining to the polio vaccine. Let $X = 1$ if people receive the polio vaccine (otherwise $X = 0$), and let $Y = 1$ if people suffer paralytic polio (otherwise $Y = 0$). According to the information provided earlier, 201,229 subjects did not receive a vaccine injection, and 200,745 subjects received the polio vaccine. Among those who received the injection, 0.016% later developed paralytic polio. Furthermore, 0.057% of those who did not receive an injection later developed paralytic polio. These results are modified and presented as a 2×2 contingency table in Table 3.4. The correlation between incidence of paralytic polio and injection can also be calculated by the formula

$$\phi = \frac{bc - ad}{\sqrt{(a+c)(b+d)(a+b)(c+d)}},$$

assuming $(a+c)(b+d)(a+b)(c+d) \neq 0$.

TABLE 3.4
2 × 2 Contingency Table Pertaining to Polio Vaccine
Injection and Paralytic Polio

	No Paralytic Polio $(Y = 0)$	Paralytic Polio $(Y = 1)$	Total
Injection $(X = 1)$	$200,713 = a$	$32 = b$	$200,745 = (a+b)$
No injection $(X = 0)$	$201,114 = c$	$115 = d$	$201,229 = (c+d)$
Total	$401,827 = (a+c)$	$147 = (b+d)$	$401,974 = a+b+c+d$

$$\phi = \frac{bc - ad}{\sqrt{(a+c)(b+d)(a+b)(c+d)}} = \frac{32 \times 201,114 - 200,713 \times 115}{\sqrt{401,827 \times 147 \times 200,745 \times 201,229}} = -0.01$$

Letters such as a, b, c, and d represent frequencies in each cell. By substituting the letters with the correspondent frequencies, we obtain $\phi = -0.01$, which suggests that people who receive the polio vaccine tend not to suffer paralytic polio.

Although the theoretical range of Pearson's r varies from 1 to -1, the range of ϕ in absolute value is often less than 1, unless $p_X = p_Y = 0.5$, where both p_X and p_Y are the proportions of people scoring 1 on X and Y, respectively. It is likely for ϕ to be 1, but not -1, when $p_X = p_Y \neq 0.5$. In contrast, it is likely for ϕ to be -1, but not 1, when $p_X = q_Y \neq 0.5$. Both q_Y and q_X are the proportions of people scoring 0 on Y and X, respectively.

Assuming $p_X q_X p_Y q_Y \neq 0$, Carroll (1961) has shown the maximum value of ϕ is reflected by either $[(p_X q_Y)/(p_Y q_X)]^{1/2}$ when $p_X < p_Y$ or $[(p_Y q_X)/(p_X q_Y)]^{1/2}$ when $p_Y < p_X$. From these formulas, we can infer that the greater the difference between p_X and p_Y, the smaller the maximum ϕ. For instance, the maximum value of ϕ is about 0.53 when $p_X = 0.4$ and $p_Y = 0.7$. In contrast, the maximum value of ϕ drastically decreases to 0.07 when $p_X = 0.01$ and $p_Y = 0.7$.

Spearman Rank-Order Correlation, r_{rank}

The Spearman rank-order correlation (r_{rank}) is another special case of Pearson's r. This index assesses the relationship between two sets of true ranked scores (e.g., $1, 2, 3, \ldots, n$). The ranks of a variable can be directly assigned or indirectly derived by ranking an ordinal variable (whatever the measurement units are). An example of its use is provided using the data presented in Table 3.5, which are the results from a judge who assigns ranks of 1 to 20 to 20 figure skaters based on technical as well as artistic performance (where 1 stands for the highest performance and 20 stands for the poorest performance). The relationship between technical skill and artistic skill can be assessed simply with the Pearson's r formula. Assuming there are no tied ranks, r_{rank} can also be calculated by

$$r_{\text{rank}} = 1 - \frac{6 \sum d^2}{n^3 - n},$$

where d is the difference between X and Y. However, this simplified formula cannot correctly calculate the correlation if tied ranks exist. The Pearson's r formula should be applied instead.

TABLE 3.5

Ranks of 20 Figure Skaters on Technical Performance (X) and
Artistic Performance (Y) by a Judge

Technical Performance	Artistic Performance	X^2	Y^2	XY	$d^2 = (X - Y)^2$
1	6	1	36	6	25
2	4	4	16	8	4
3	2	9	4	6	1
4	3	16	9	12	1
5	1	25	1	5	16
6	5	36	25	30	1
7	7	49	49	49	0
8	9	64	81	72	1
9	12	81	144	108	9
10	10	100	100	100	0
11	8	121	64	88	9
12	11	144	121	132	1
13	13	169	169	169	0
14	15	196	225	210	1
15	14	225	196	210	1
16	17	256	289	272	1
17	18	289	324	306	1
18	16	324	256	288	4
19	19	361	361	361	0
20	20	400	400	400	0

$\sum X = 210 \quad \sum Y = 210 \quad \sum X^2 = 2870 \quad \sum Y^2 = 2870 \quad \sum XY = 2832 \quad \sum d^2 = 76$

$$r_{rank} = \frac{2832 - \frac{210 \times 210}{20}}{\sqrt{2870 - \frac{210^2}{20}} \sqrt{2870 - \frac{210^2}{20}}} = 0.94 \qquad r_{rank} = 1 - \frac{6 \sum d^2}{n^3 - n} = 1 - \frac{6 \times 76}{20^3 - 20} = 0.94$$

NOTE: r_{rank} on the left side of the table is calculated based on the Pearson's r computation formula.

Similar to the previous correlation indexes, the null hypothesis test of $\rho_{rank} = 0$ can be conducted by

$$t = \frac{r_{rank}}{\sqrt{(1 - r_{rank}^2)/(n - 2)}}, \qquad df = n - 2,$$

when the sample size is $19 \leq n < 30$. However, the test of $\rho_{rank} = 0$ can be more accurately conducted by $z = r_{rank}(n - 1)^{1/2}$ if $n > 35$ (Kendall & Gibbons, 1990).

Because the sampling distribution of r_{rank} is not distributed as the t or z distribution when the sample size is small, exact critical values should be used. These values can be found in many statistics books such as Kendall and Gibbons (1990, pp. 206–213). Note that major statistical packages such as SAS® or SPSS® do not take the sample size into consideration and use the t distribution to conduct the null hypothesis tests. For example, according to the α of 0.05, two-tailed, any r_{rank} calculated from a sample of 10 subjects should be greater than 0.648 in order to reject the null hypothesis of $\rho_{rank} = 0$. However, the null hypothesis is rejected when $r_{rank} > 0.632$ if the t distribution is employed. Therefore, results of the significance test from SAS® or SPSS® are not exact when the sample size is small and should be used with caution.

True Versus Artificially Converted Scores

As noted earlier, r_{pb}, ϕ, and r_{rank} are special cases of Pearson's r. However, Pearson's r based on two continuous variables will not be the same as r_{pb}, ϕ, and r_{rank} if the raw scores of one or two continuous variables are artificially converted into either a dichotomous variable or a set of ranks. In general, Pearson's r calculated based on two continuous variables tends to be greater than r_{rank}, r_{pb}, and ϕ if the latter are calculated based on ranked scores or dichotomous scores, which are artificially converted from the same two continuous variables. The decrease in the size of r_{rank}, r_{pb}, and ϕ in the above example is generally attributed to a loss of information and precision when artificially converting one or two continuous variables into ranked or dichotomous variables.

As an example of this, the values of two continuous variables, X and Y, are presented in the first two columns of Table 3.6. The third and the fourth columns are the ranks artificially converted from the raw scores of X and Y. It is clearly shown that the size of Pearson's r (0.22) based on the raw scores is notably greater than that of r_{rank} (0.12) based on the converted ranked scores.

It is important to note that the types of relationships assessed by r_{pb}, ϕ, and r_{rank} may change contingent upon the nature of the data. If these indexes are calculated based on true dichotomous categories or two true sets of ranks, they are gauging the *linear* relationship between variables just as Pearson's r does. Whatever formulas are applied to calculate r_{pb}, ϕ, or r_{rank} under these circumstances, their results will

TABLE 3.6

Difference Between Pearson's r and the Spearman
Rank-Order Correlation Should Raw Scores of
Continuous Variables Be Converted Into Two
Sets of Ranked Scores

X	Y	Rank of X	Rank of Y
4	10	25.0	10.5
6	4	23.5	24.0
6	6	23.5	19.0
8	8	21.0	14.0
8	8	21.0	14.0
8	8	21.0	14.0
10	12	18.0	7.5
10	12	18.0	7.5
10	6	18.0	19.0
12	6	14.0	19.0
12	5	14.0	22.0
12	16	14.0	4.0
12	16	14.0	4.0
12	8	14.0	14.0
14	8	10.0	14.0
14	10	10.0	10.5
14	6	10.0	19.0
16	18	7.5	2.0
16	16	7.5	4.0
18	12	4.5	7.5
18	4	4.5	24.0
18	19	4.5	1.0
18	12	4.5	7.5
19	4	1.5	24.0
19	6	1.5	19.0

Pearson's $r = 0.22$	Spearman rank-order correlation $= 0.12$

NOTE: Rank 1 is assigned to the highest value of X and Y. If there are ties, the average of the rank is used.

be the same as those calculated by the Pearson's r formula. However, r_{pb}, ϕ, and r_{rank} become measures of *monotonic* relationships if they are calculated based on artificially converted scores or ranks. A positive/negative monotonic relationship describes both variables moving toward same/opposite directions together in a nonlinear form.

In the practical world, researchers may actually want to convert the raw scores of continuous variables. For instance, the existence of outliers (i.e., extreme raw scores) may distort the relationship between variables. The distortion can be remedied if researchers convert raw scores into ranks. The conversion may also be necessary if raw scores are mixed with nonspecific values. For example, a few respondents in a survey do not write down their actual ages. Instead, they jot down "older than 50" or "older than 60." As a result, these respondents are dropped from the analysis. If researchers would like to include these subjects, all the raw scores and nonspecified values can be converted into ranks or two mutually exclusively categories.

Often, we are uncertain if the Pearson's r formula should be used when two variables are measured at the ordinal level (i.e., the scores only reflect a crude degree of an attribute). The solution to this dilemma may only be reached after debating whether the variable should be viewed as an ordinal variable or a continuous variable. For instance, the measures of life satisfaction and job satisfaction can arguably be viewed as either ordinal or continuous variables. If we are convinced that both of them are continuous variables, their relationship can be measured by Pearson's r. If we argue that both of them are true ordinal variables, both measures can logically be rescaled into ranked scores first. After that, the Pearson's r formula is applied accordingly.

Biserial Coefficient, r_{bis}

If a variable X has an underlying normal distribution, but is artificially measured as a dichotomous variable (e.g., pass vs. fail or light vs. heavy), its original relationship with another continuous variable (e.g., SAT score or protein intake) can be *estimated* by the biserial coefficient (r_{bis}). Putting this in terms from the previous section, the biserial coefficient is an index that estimates what the relationship between X and Y would be if X were not artificially converted into a dichotomous variable. In contrast, the dichotomous variable in the point-biserial correlation is truly binary (death vs. survival or male vs. female).

For instance, an industrial engineer is interested in finding out the relationship between the operational condition of a machine and hours of operation. The engineer first assesses the condition of 20 plastic injection machines and labels them as in either good (coded 2) or poor (coded 1) condition, although the operational condition is actually a continuous variable that is assumed to have a normal distribution. Records of hours of operation over a week are retrieved, and the data are reproduced in Table 3.7a. In practice, researchers often conduct either an independent two-sample t test ($t = 2.98$) or a point-biserial correlation (-0.58). Both results suggest that machines in poor operational condition have higher hours of operation than those in good operational condition. The negative relationship reveals that the better the operational condition of the machine, the fewer the hours of operation.

In contrast to the above, the researcher may be interested in estimating the relationship between operational function and hours of operation if the former is not artificially dichotomized. This estimated correlation, the biserial correlation, could be derived by

$$r_{\text{bis}} = \frac{\overline{Y}_2 - \overline{Y}_1}{s_Y}\left(\frac{n_2 n_1}{\lambda(n_1 + n_2)^2}\right),$$

where $\overline{Y}_1$ and $\overline{Y}_2$ are the means of Y for samples 1 and 2; n_1 and n_2 are the sizes of samples 1 and 2; s_Y is the standard deviation of all scores on Y; and λ is the ordinate of the standardized normal distribution at $n_2/(n_1 + n_2)$, proportion of subjects in sample 2 (λ can be obtained by the SPSS® syntax included in Appendix 3).

TABLE 3.7a
Operational Condition (X) and Hours of
Operation Over a Week (Y)

X	Y	X	Y
1	18	2	10
1	10	2	7
1	16	2	12
1	20	2	16
1	16	2	13
1	16	2	7
1	12	2	7
1	15	2	14
1	12	2	10
1	14	2	12
$\overline{Y}_1 = 14.9$, $s_1^2 = 8.989$		$\overline{Y}_2 = 10.8$, $s_2^2 = 9.956$	

NOTE: $\overline{Y} = 12.85$, $s_y = 3.66$. Operational condition (X) is coded as Poor = 1 and Good = 2.

Following the above formula,

$$r_{\text{bis}} = \frac{10.8 - 14.9}{3.66} \left(\frac{10 \times 10}{0.398942 \times (10 + 10)^2} \right) = -0.70,$$

which is noticeably larger than r_{pb}, -0.57. The mathematical relationship between r_{bis} and r_{pb} is summarized as

$$r_{\text{bis}} = r_{\text{pb}} \sqrt{\frac{n_2 n_1 (n_1 + n_2 - 1)}{\lambda^2 (n_1 + n_2)^3}}.$$

Because

$$\sqrt{\frac{n_2 n_1 (n_1 + n_2 - 1)}{\lambda^2 (n_1 + n_2)^3}} \geq 1.25,$$

r_{bis} is always greater than r_{pb} (Glass & Hopkins, 1996). That is, the relationship between two continuous variables with bivariate normal distributions becomes smaller if one of them is artificially dichotomized. Under certain circumstances (e.g., the distribution of a continuous variable is bimodal or platykurtic; McNemar, 1969), r_{bis} can even be greater than 1.

Tetrachoric Coefficient, r_{tet}

If researchers artificially dichotomize two continuous variables with a bivariate normal distribution, the relationship between these two dichotomized variables is referred to as a tetrachoric correlation (r_{tet}). Similar to r_{bis}, r_{tet} is merely an estimation of the relationship should the variables not be artificially dichotomized and assuming both variables have a bivariate normal distribution. Modified from the example described in the preceding section, the variable of hours of operation is artificially dichotomized as short hours (if the machine is in operation less than 12.5 hours) or long hours (if the machine is in operation more than 12.5 hours). The results using the two dichotomized variables are summarized in the 2×2 contingency table shown in Table 3.7b.

The tetrachoric correlation can be computed by

$$r_{\text{tet}} = \frac{bc - ad}{\lambda_X \lambda_Y n^2},$$

TABLE 3.7b
2 × 2 Contingency Table Pertaining to Operational
Condition (X) and Hours of Operation (Y)

	Short (Y = 0)	Long (Y = 1)	Total
Good (X = 1)	7 = a	3 = b	10 = (a + b)
Poor (X = 0)	3 = c	7 = d	10 = (c + d)
Total	10 = (a + c)	10 = (b + d)	20 = a + b + c + d

NOTE: Operational condition (X) is coded as Good = 1 and Poor = 0. Hours of operation (Y) shorter than 12.5 are labeled as short and coded as 0; otherwise, they are labeled as long and coded as 1.

where n is the total sample size; λ_X is the ordinate of the standardized normal distribution at $(a+b)/(a+b+c+d)$, proportion of subjects obtaining $X = 1$; and λ_Y is the ordinate of the standardized normal distribution at $(b+d)/(a+b+c+d)$, proportion of subjects obtaining $Y = 1$. Substituting the data in Table 3.7b, the tetrachoric correlation between operational condition and hours of operation is calculated as

$$r_{\text{tet}} = \frac{3 \times 3 - 7 \times 7}{0.398942 \times 0.398942 \times 20^2} = -0.63.$$

Comparing r_{tet}, ϕ calculated based on the same data is much smaller ($\phi = -0.4$). It should be emphasized that r_{tet} would not reasonably estimate the relationship unless the sample size is above 400 (Glass & Hopkins, 1996). As stressed earlier, continuous variables should not be artificially converted unless there are practical or compelling reasons to do so. Both r_{bis} and r_{tet} are rarely used in practice, and they should be used with caution because they are hypothetical correlations. Readers who are interested in null hypothesis tests of r_{bis} or r_{tet} can refer to Glass and Hopkins (pp. 368–369).

Eta Coefficient, η

The eta coefficient (η) is an index assessing the association between a multichotomous variable X with k mutually exclusive categories and a variable Y with interval or ratio scores. In contrast to the other correlation indexes discussed so far, the η coefficient only describes the strength of a relationship between variables. The assessment of the direction of the relationship is irrelevant because the categories of the multichotomous variable generally do not reflect any order sequence (e.g., political parties). Therefore, the η coefficient can also be used to describe the curvilinear relationship between a multichotomous variable and a variable measured at the interval or ratio level.

The η coefficient, also referred to as a correlation ratio, is usually applied in the context of analysis of variance (ANOVA). For example, a biologist investigates if there is any mean difference on growth rate among three types of viruses. The researcher monitors the growth rates of 10 cases in each type and records the findings in Table 3.8. Results of the ANOVA reported in Table 3.8 reveal that there are significant mean differences in growth rate among the three types of viruses. In other words, there is a significant association between type

TABLE 3.8
Growth Rates of Three Types of Viruses and Results
of Analysis of Variance

Virus A	Virus B	Virus C
2.5	3.2	3.5
2.6	3.4	3.2
2.7	2.6	3.0
3.2	3.2	3.0
2.8	3.9	3.6
2.4	2.7	2.9
2.1	3.1	3.3
2.0	2.9	4.1
2.5	3.4	3.2
2.2	2.9	3.5
$n_A = 10$	$n_B = 10$	$n_C = 10$
$\overline{Y}_A = 2.50$	$\overline{Y}_B = 3.13$	$\overline{Y}_C = 3.33$
$s_A = 0.36$	$s_B = 0.38$	$s_C = 0.36$

ANOVA

Growth Rate

	Sum of Squares	df	Mean Square	F	Sig.
Between groups	3.753	2	1.876	13.987	0.000
Within groups	3.622	27	0.134		
Total	7.375	29			

TABLE 3.9
Relationship Between Growth Rate and Type of Virus

Virus	Growth Rate	Virus	Growth Rate	Virus	Growth Rate
2.50	2.5	3.13	3.2	3.33	3.5
2.50	2.6	3.13	3.4	3.33	3.2
2.50	2.7	3.13	2.6	3.33	3.0
2.50	3.2	3.13	3.2	3.33	3.0
2.50	2.8	3.13	3.9	3.33	3.6
2.50	2.4	3.13	2.7	3.33	2.9
2.50	2.1	3.13	3.1	3.33	3.3
2.50	2.0	3.13	2.9	3.33	4.1
2.50	2.5	3.13	3.4	3.33	3.2
2.50	2.2	3.13	2.9	3.33	3.5

NOTE: Virus A is coded as 2.5 ($\overline{Y}_A$), virus B is coded as 3.13 ($\overline{Y}_B$), and virus C is coded as 3.33 ($\overline{Y}_C$).

of virus and growth rate. This association is assessed by

$$\eta = \sqrt{\frac{SS_{\text{between}}}{SS_{\text{total}}}}.$$

Based on the ANOVA results, $SS_{\text{between}} = 3.753$, $SS_{\text{total}} = 7.375$, and $\eta = 0.71$, which is significantly different from 0 according to the observed F value in Table 3.8 ($F = 13.99$, $p < 0.05$, two-tailed).

According to Wherry (1984), η is also a special case of Pearson's r if the value of X of each case within each category is substituted by the correspondent mean of Y. Following the above example, X is coded as 2.50, 3.13, and 3.33 for virus A, virus B, and virus C, respectively. According to the Pearson's r formula and the rearranged data shown in Table 3.9, we can obtain $|r| = 0.71$, which is exactly the same as the value of η except for the rounding error.

Other Special Cases of Pearson's r

Recall from Table 1.1 that there are four additional special cases of Pearson's r. These lesser known correlations have been elaborated by Wherry (1984) and can be used to measure (1) a relationship between an ordinal variable and a continuous variable, r_{RI}; (2) a relationship between a dichotomous variable and an ordinal variable, r_{DR}; (3) an association between a multichotomous (i.e., more than two categories) variable and a dichotomous variable, r_{MD}; and (4) an association between a multichotomous variable and an ordinal variable, r_{MR}. Unlike the correlations described previously, there are no specific labels designated for these correlations. In the remainder of this chapter, we will briefly show how these four correlations are computed and how the null hypothesis tests are conducted, based primarily on Wherry's seminal work.

Without any manipulation of data, both r_{RI} and r_{DR} can simply be computed by the Pearson's r equation. In addition, the null hypothesis test of $\rho = 0$ for r_{RI} and r_{DR} can be conducted by $z = r_{RI}(n-1)^{1/2}$ and $z = r_{DR}(n-1)^{1/2}$ when $n > 30$. To compute either r_{MD} or r_{MR}, a pseudo-coding is required for the multichotomous variable. This type of coding procedure was described earlier when calculating the η coefficient. Suppose Y is either a dichotomous or a rank variable and X is a multichotomous variable with k categories. Let the value of X for each case within each category be substituted by the correspondent mean of Y. After that, r_{MD} and r_{MR} can be computed by the Pearson's r formula. Because k categories in the multichotomous variable can be arranged in any order, the direction of r_{MD} and r_{MR} based on the Pearson's r formula is not relevant. We will use their absolute values to represent the strength of the association between two variables. The appropriate null hypothesis test for r_{MD} is $\chi^2 = n(r_{MD}^2)$, $df = k - 1$, and the correspondent test for r_{MR} is $\chi^2 = (n-1)(r_{MR}^2)$, $df = k - 1$.

These special cases of Pearson's r can provide both researchers and practitioners with additional tools to help in the identification and understanding of relationships between variables. This capability can be extended further with the applications presented in Chapter 4.

4. APPLICATIONS OF PEARSON'S r

As briefly described in Chapter 1, correlation indexes can be applied to various purposes. In the last two chapters, we have examined how Pearson's r is used to provide descriptive information about a relationship between variables, as well as to conduct various null hypothesis tests, including tests of $\rho = 0$, $\rho = $ a specific nonzero value, equality between two or more independent ρs, and equality between two dependent ρs. In this chapter, we will introduce other important applications that are useful both in research and in practice. Specifically, we will discuss the following applications: effect size, power analysis, meta-analysis, utility analysis, reliability estimates, and validation.

Power analysis, meta-analysis, and utility analysis are extended applications of effect size, and the latter two topics are core components in measurement theory.

Application I: Effect Size

Pearson's r has been used as one of the effect size indexes. Cohen (1988, p. 8) broadly defined effect size as "the degree to which the phenomenon is present in the population" or "the degree to which the null hypothesis is false." Effect size in the correlational context is referred to as the strength of association between two variables. There are at least three types of effect sizes calculated by the Pearson correlation: r^2 (Murphy & Myors, 1998), $r/(1 - r^2)^{1/2}$ or $r^2/(1 - r^2)$ (Rosenthal, 1991), and r (Cohen, 1988). Although we will use Pearson's r as the effect size when we discuss applications of meta-analysis and utility analysis, it is important to understand the meaning of $r^2/(1 - r^2)$ here.

There are two components in the index of $r^2/(1 - r^2)$: r^2 in the numerator and $1 - r^2$ in the denominator. The value of $1 - r^2$ is referred to as the coefficient of nondetermination. Suppose the correlation coefficient of candy consumption and weight gain is 0.5. The value of $1 - r^2$, 0.75, suggests that there is 75% of variance that candy consumption and weight gain do not have in common. In contrast, r^2 refers to the 25% of variance shared by candy consumption and weight gain. The index of $r^2/(1 - r^2)$, therefore, can be conceptualized as the ratio of signal/noise (Rothenthal, 1991). The larger this ratio, the more signal relative to noise.

Many researchers attempt to verbally indicate the effect size of their correlations by using such phrases as "highly significant" or by showing a "moderate relationship between X and Y." Cohen (1988) is probably the most often cited scholar when researchers attempt to describe the size of a correlation. Although Cohen provided a conventional frame of reference pertaining to small (0.1), moderate (0.3), and large (0.5) correlation, he clearly pointed out that these adjectives are "relative, not only to each other, but to the area of behavioral science or even more particularly to the specific content and research method being employed in any given investigation" (p. 25).

A statement such as "*only* 10% of variance of Y is explained by X" somewhat implies that a small relationship is not practically important. In contrast to this perspective, a small correlation can be very impressive, as well as extremely important for various reasons. Recall that Dr. Jonas Salk's experiment only showed a correlation of -0.01 between polio vaccine and paralytic polio (99.99% of the variance is *not* explained by the polio vaccine)! We will revisit this issue later when we discuss the application of Pearson's r to utility analysis.

Application II: Power Analysis

Researchers often want to estimate how many subjects they will need in order to find a significant correlation with a particular level of statistical power. Statistical power is defined as the probability of accepting the alternative hypothesis when the alternative hypothesis is true. Although perfect statistical power will not help researchers reveal phenomena that do not exist (i.e., zero effect), low statistical power tends to guarantee that researchers will not find the phenomena that do exist. With this in mind, it only makes sense that researchers should strive for high statistical power (say at least 0.8) so that their studies are sensitive enough to assure the success of their research.

Cohen (1962) reported an average power of 0.18 for detecting a Pearson's r of 0.20, 0.48 for a Pearson's r of 0.40, and 0.83 for a Pearson's r of 0.60 in the 1960 volume of the *Journal of Abnormal and Social Psychology*. Given that most research only exhibits an effect size of around 0.4 in the above volume, the researchers only had less than a 50% chance of accepting the alternative hypothesis when the alternative hypothesis was true. Their chance of success was even worse than that expected from flipping a coin! Sedlmeier and Gigerenzer (1989) took a similar approach to study statistical power based on the 1984 volume of the *Journal of Abnormal Psychology*. They reported an average power of only 0.37 for detecting a Pearson's r of 0.40! It should be noted that the small effect sizes noted above may not be representative of other fields.

It is hoped that these two cases will convince readers to stress statistical power when preparing for future studies. Statistical power, holding other elements (e.g., linearity assumption) constant, is a function of effect size, sample size, and alpha level. If researchers determine the effect size, the sample size can be easily estimated under a certain alpha level and statistical power. In the following three sections, we will describe how to estimate the number of subjects needed to achieve a statistical power of 0.8, the minimum goal researchers attempt to achieve (Murphy & Myors, 1998) when conducting three forms of null hypothesis tests involving Pearson's r.

Subjects Needed When Testing $\rho \neq 0$

Suppose we expect a Pearson's r of 0.2 estimated from prior research or pilot studies, holding other parameters constant without violating the assumption of Pearson's r. The number of subjects needed to achieve the level 0.8 statistical power can be approximated by using the following formulas (Howell, 1997):

$$n = \frac{(2.8016)^2}{r^2} + 1 \qquad (\alpha = 0.05, \text{ two-tailed}),$$

$$n = \frac{(2.4865)^2}{r^2} + 1 \qquad (\alpha = 0.05, \text{ one-tailed}),$$

$$n = \frac{(3.4174)^2}{r^2} + 1 \qquad (\alpha = 0.01, \text{ two-tailed}),$$

and

$$n = \frac{(3.1679)^2}{r^2} + 1 \qquad (\alpha = 0.01, \text{one-tailed}).$$

Substituting 0.2 for r in the above formulas, we would have an 80% chance of rejecting the null hypothesis of $\rho = 0$ with approximately 197 subjects ($\alpha = 0.05$, two-tailed) or 293 subjects ($\alpha = 0.01$, two-tailed). A more accurate general formula to estimate the number of subjects required for the above case is too complex to include here. Readers who are interested in this topic should refer to Appendix A in Murphy and Myors (1998).

Subjects Needed When Testing $\rho \neq a$ Nonzero Value

A researcher develops a salesperson selection inventory that is used to predict future sales performance. Most salesperson selection inventories in the current testing market have demonstrated an average correlation of 0.3 with sales performance. According to a pilot study, the researcher expects the newly developed inventory to outperform the conventional tests and anticipates the relationship between test and sales performance to be around 0.4. How many subjects should the researcher recruit to have an 80% chance of rejecting the null hypothesis should the correlation be 0.4? Before finding out the expected sample size, the researcher first needs to determine the possible difference between an observed Fisher's z_r and the specific Fisher's z_r with which to compare it. Let the difference between two z_rs be denoted as D. The expected sample size with a power of 0.8 can be easily estimated based on the formulas described below. These formulas are developed according to a procedure described by Trattner and O'Leary (1980). Given $\alpha = 0.05$,

$$n = \frac{(2.8016)^2}{D^2} + 3 \text{ (two-tailed)} \quad \text{and} \quad n = \frac{(2.4865)^2}{D^2} + 3 \text{ (one-tailed)};$$

given $\alpha = 0.01$,

$$n = \frac{(3.4174)^2}{D^2} + 3 \text{ (two-tailed)} \quad \text{and} \quad n = \frac{(3.1679)^2}{D^2} + 3 \text{ (one-tailed)}.$$

Derivations of the above numerators can be found in Trattner and O'Leary (1980).

Following the above example, the null hypothesis is $\rho = 0.3$, and the alternative hypothesis is $\rho > 0.3$. Based on the researcher's expectation, D would be 0.114, which is the difference between 0.424 and 0.31. Accordingly, the researcher should plan to recruit either 479 subjects ($\alpha = 0.05$) or 776 subjects ($\alpha = 0.01$) in order to have an 80% chance of rejecting the null hypothesis.

Subjects Needed When Testing $\rho_1 \neq \rho_2$

Researchers and practitioners often examine if there is any difference between two independent correlations derived from two samples. For example, assume a political consultant hypothesizes that the relationship between preference for a political party and amount of donations to the party is different between males and females. How many males and females are needed in this study so that there is an 80% chance of the consultant's rejecting the null hypothesis of $\rho_1 = \rho_2$?

The consultant first needs to determine the possible difference between two Fisher's z_rs. Let the difference be denoted as D. The expected sample size with a power of 0.8 can be calculated after the sample size of group 1, n_1, is determined. The n_1 can be arbitrarily decided or can be decided on the basis of any information available to the consultant. As shown in the following formulas, which are modified from Trattner and O'Leary (1980), the sample size of group 2 is easily estimated should the values of D and n_1 be chosen.

Given $\alpha = 0.05$,

$$n_2 = \frac{(2.8016)^2}{D^2 - \frac{(2.8016)^2}{n_1 - 3}} + 3 \text{ (two-tailed)} \quad \text{and}$$

$$n_2 = \frac{(2.4865)^2}{D^2 - \frac{(2.4865)^2}{n_1 - 3}} + 3 \text{ (one-tailed)};$$

given $\alpha = 0.01$,

$$n_2 = \frac{(3.4174)^2}{D^2 - \frac{(3.4174)^2}{n_1 - 3}} + 3 \text{ (two-tailed)} \quad \text{and}$$

$$n_2 = \frac{(3.1679)^2}{D^2 - \frac{(3.1679)^2}{n_1 - 3}} + 3 \text{ (one-tailed)}.$$

Suppose the consultant estimates the difference between two Fisher's z_rs as 0.4 and determines the sample size of group 1, n_1, as 100. Given the two-tailed test, the consultant should plan to recruit either 103 subjects ($\alpha = 0.05$) or 298 subjects ($\alpha = 0.01$) in order to have an 80% chance of rejecting the null hypothesis.

Note that the sample size in the smaller group sets a limit for achieving a desired power (Trattner & O'Leary, 1980). The following example explains what Trattner and O'Leary meant. Suppose n_1 is changed to 50 in the above example, the consultant needs to recruit either -1119 subjects ($\alpha = 0.05$) or -129 subjects ($\alpha = 0.01$). These estimates, while nonsensical, do allow us to conclude that, in this case, adequate power cannot be achieved. As a general rule of thumb, the smaller the D values, the larger the sample sizes required for n_1. When the D values reach around 0.25 to 0.35, approximately 100 subjects for group 1 are needed.

Application III: Meta-Analysis

Meta-analysis is a quantitative approach that integrates research findings across studies (e.g., using an average effect size to summarize the general findings). Before researchers conduct a meta-analysis, they first review the literature and then retrieve published as well as unpublished studies that contain the same information pertaining to the topics they are interested in. After that, they extract statistics found in the studies and convert the statistics into an index of effect size. The bare bones of a meta-analysis is to calculate a weighted average effect size. Weights can be sample sizes or other values that are inversely proportional to the variance of the statistic. An in-depth discussion pertaining to the approaches and procedures of conducting a meta-analysis are beyond the scope of this monograph. Readers who are interested in this topic should consult Rosenthal (1991) or Hunter and Schmidt (1990).

In this section, we will use Alliger and Janak's (1989) study of training outcomes to illustrate how Pearson's r plays a critical role in meta-analysis. Alliger and Janak attempted to estimate the actual relationships among four types of training outcomes assessed in business settings: reaction, learning, behavior, and outcome. Reaction criteria refer to trainees' affective reactions (i.e., whether they liked the training or not). Learning criteria are defined as the amount of knowledge or skill trainees actually obtain from training programs. Behavior criteria refer to how much of the learned skills or knowledge trainees actually transfer into their daily task environment. Outcome criteria focus on the actual benefits to corporations that spend money to train employees.

Alliger and Janak reported all the meta-analyzed correlations in Table 3 of their article. We will choose only two sets of correlations (reaction-learning and reaction-behavior) to replicate their findings here. As shown in Table 4.1, six studies reported the relationship between reaction and learning, and four studies reported the relationship between reaction and behavior. The sample size of each meta-analyzed study is also included in the table.

Recall from Chapter 2 that sampling distributions of Pearson's r are either negatively or positively skewed when the population ρ is not equal to 0. Because of this special feature of Pearson's r, an average correlation based on the rs tends to underestimate a nonzero population correlation coefficient, ρ. The extent of this bias increases if the size of the population ρ increases, if the correlations are heterogeneous, or if the number of correlations to be averaged decreases (Strube, 1988). To eliminate this problem, all Pearson's rs are transformed into Fisher's z_rs (shown in the fourth column in Table 4.1),

TABLE 4.1

Correlations of Reaction With Learning and Reaction With Behavior
Based on the Data Reported by Alliger and Janak (1989)

			Reaction-Learning		
Study	Pearson's r	Sample (n)	Fisher's z_r	$z_r \times (n-3)$	$r \times n$
1	0.79	105	1.071432	109.286	82.95
2	0.50	50	0.549306	25.81739	25
3	0.35	118	0.365444	42.02603	41.3
4	0.17	57	0.171667	9.27	9.69
5	0.07	256	0.070115	17.73901	17.92
6	−0.03	1259	−0.03001	−37.6913	−37.77
		Average correlation, $\bar{r}$		0.09	0.07

			Reaction-Behavior		
Study	Pearson's r	Sample (n)	Fisher's z_r	$z_r \times (n-3)$	$r \times n$
1	0.12	103	0.120581	12.0581	12.36
2	0.04	256	0.040021	10.1254	10.24
3	0.06	60	0.060072	3.424113	3.6
4	0.01	173	0.01	1.700057	1.73
		Average correlation, $\bar{r}$		0.05	0.05

assuming the correlations to be averaged are from the same population. Because there are k studies involved in a meta-analysis, the average $\bar{z}_r$ is weighted by $(n_k - 3)$ (shown in the fifth column), which is inversely proportional to the variance of z_r, $1/(n_k - 3)$. The average $\bar{z}_r$ based on the inverse of the variance $(n_k - 3)$ can be computed by

$$\bar{z}_r = \frac{(n_1 - 3)z_{r_1} + (n_2 - 3)z_{r_2} + \cdots + (n_k - 3)z_{r_k}}{(n_1 - 3) + (n_2 - 3) + \cdots + (n_k - 3)}.$$

After $\bar{z}_r$ is obtained, it can be converted back to $\bar{r}$ by

$$\bar{r} = \frac{e^{2\bar{z}_r} - 1}{e^{2\bar{z}_r} + 1}.$$

As shown in Table 4.1, the average correlations between reaction and learning and reaction and behavior are 0.09 and 0.05, respectively. If we follow Hunter and Schmidt's (1990) procedure by only averaging Pearson's rs weighted by n_k (shown in the sixth column), the average correlations are 0.07 and 0.05, respectively, which are exactly those reported by Alliger and Janak (1989).

Application IV: Utility Analysis

Utility analysis is a cost-accounting method, which estimates the benefit of interventions such as safety and health training in corporations in dollar terms. For instance, the food service and retail industries continuously face rapid turnover among their employees. There are many explicit as well as hidden expenses associated with employee turnover. Suppose a retention program is developed and implemented to alleviate the problem. The use of effect sizes or statistics derived from data analysis is limited when it comes to communicating the monetary effect of this retention program. Utility analysis can be an extremely handy and powerful way to communicate with involved parties regarding the potential economic gains.

Let us use a personnel selection program described by Cascio (1991, pp. 191–194) to demonstrate the role of Pearson's r in a utility analysis. Suppose a company uses a computer programming test to select job candidates. The monetary net gain (ΔU) of the selection test per applicant can be described as

$$\Delta U = \left(\frac{N_s}{N_{app}}\right)(SD_y)(r_{xy})\left(\frac{\lambda}{SR}\right) - C,$$

where N_s is the number of selected candidates, N_{app} is the number of test-takers, r_{xy} refers to the correlation between test score (X) and job performance (Y) in the a priori population, SD_y is the standard deviation of Y in the dollar scale, and λ stands for the ordinate of the normal curve at the cutoff score on the X. Job candidates are selected if their test scores are above the cutoff score, C is the cost per test-taker, and SR represents the percentage of job candidates who are selected from the applicant pool.

The above formula can further be modified to evaluate the effect of an intervention program such as skill training (X) on job performance (Y). The formula is

$$\Delta U = (N_{trainees})(SD_y)(r_{xy}) - (C \times N_{trainees}).$$

When $SD_y = \$15,000$, $r_{xy} = 0.1$, $N_{\text{trainees}} = 100$, and C per trainee = $500.00, the annual net gain of implementing the skill training program turns out to be $100,000.00! A correlation of 0.1 may be small according to the conventional frame of reference (Cohen, 1988), yet the annual monetary return can be quite impressive!

Following the above formulas, an increase in r_{xy} is associated with an increase in the monetary net gain. In other words, the company would see a great return on investment (cost of test administration or training) when a valid selection test or training program is implemented. Practically, N, r_{xy}, λ, C, and SR are readily available, although SD_y is often difficult to estimate. There are several approaches proposed to estimate SD_y. Because the topic of estimating SD_y is beyond the scope of this monograph, interested readers should refer to Cascio (1991).

Application V: Reliability Estimates

The concept of correlation is very important in understanding and estimating reliability. We do not intend that our coverage in the next two sections constitute an in-depth discussion of these core components in the theory of measurement. Rather, we stress the role of Pearson's r in assessing reliability and validity. Readers who are interested in the special treatment of validity and reliability are encouraged to consult Carmines and Zeller (1979).

Pearson's r plays an indispensable role in the theory of measurement, particularly in reliability. To understand the role of Pearson's r, we need to understand the conceptual meaning of reliability. The reliability of a measure (e.g., a bathroom scale, a poll survey, a school achievement test, an employee morale survey, a physical symptoms report, etc.) can be viewed as the extent of consistency about responses to the measure. Stepping on a bathroom scale (response to the scale) repeatedly by the same person should reflect the same readings, holding all other things constant. Likewise, the reliability of a political poll means interviewees should respond to a question in a similar manner, regardless of the medium of the survey (telephone, face to face), the gender of the interviewer, or the occasion.

In reality, consistent responses to a measure are not an absolute in many disciplines. Yet, imagine how much faith we would have in theories or applications developed from the natural as well as the social sciences when one or more measurement instruments provide inconsistent readings. As a result, it is important to assess the extent to which responses toward a measure are inconsistent. Various reliability estimates such as test-retest reliability, internal consistency estimates, and alternate-forms reliability have been developed according to classical test theory to examine sources of error that produce inconsistency in responses under certain conditions (e.g., a period of time, a sample of items, a person's mood, time of day, even making mistakes in answers).

According to classical test theory, any observed score (denoted as X) in a measure consists of two components: true score (T) and random error (e). The above statement can be summarized by the equation, $X = T + e$. True score is defined as the average response of a person over the long run. Random error, responsible for inconsistent responses, results from different sources such as a certain type of question selected for a test or memory effects when people take the same test at two different times. Given that certain assumptions hold (see Carmines & Zeller, 1979), the above formula can be extended as $\sigma_X^2 = \sigma_T^2 + \sigma_e^2$. That is, the variance of the observed response (σ_X^2) equals the sum of the variance of the true score σ_T^2 and the variance of the random error σ_e^2. If the inverse of σ_X^2 is multiplied on both sides of the equation, the equation can be rewritten as

$$\frac{\sigma_X^2}{\sigma_X^2} = \frac{\sigma_T^2}{\sigma_X^2} + \frac{\sigma_e^2}{\sigma_X^2}$$

or simply as

$$1 = \frac{\sigma_T^2}{\sigma_X^2} + \frac{\sigma_e^2}{\sigma_X^2}.$$

The final form of the equation is critical for understanding the conceptual meaning of reliability. The operational definition of reliability is actually represented as the proportion of observed score variance attributed to true score variance, σ_T^2 / σ_X^2. Because variances are always greater than or equal to 0, and observed score variances are often greater than 0, the range of reliability in theory can only vary from 0 to 1.

Of the three variances described above, only the observed score variance can be obtained by administering a measure to a group of subjects. Neither the true score variance nor the random error variance can be acquired in reality because they are merely hypothetical concepts. But how can a reliability be calculated without knowing either the true score variance or the random error variance?

Suppose a test has a perfect reliability (e.g., when administered at two different times). Then a perfect correlation between the test scores should be obtained. If a measure has no reliability (i.e., the variance of observed scores is completely accounted for by the random error), a zero correlation is expected. As a result, Pearson's r becomes a useful index in practice to describe (1) the consistency between two responses derived from the same scale administered at two different times (i.e., a correlation of the same scale which is administered at two different times, used to assess the test-retest reliability), (2) the similarity between two responses derived from two similar measures (i.e., the correlation between the two similar measures, employed to gauge alternate-forms reliability), or (3) the persistence among responses toward items within a measure (e.g., the widely reported Cronbach coefficient alpha used to assess internal consistency reliability). A standardized Cronbach alpha (α) can be calculated by $k(\bar{r}_{ij})/[1 + (k-1)\bar{r}_{ij}]$, where k is the number of items in a test and $\bar{r}_{ij}$ is the average intercorrelation among test items.

When we use Pearson's r to gauge the consistency of a measure, the interpretation of the statistic r should follow the operational definition of reliability, σ_T^2/σ_X^2, described earlier. For example, a test-retest reliability of 0.8, as assessed by Pearson's r, should be interpreted as 80% of the observed score variance (σ_X^2) attributed to the true score variance (σ_T^2). In other words, 20% of the observed score variance is accounted for by the random error variance. It is a mistake to use r^2 (i.e., 0.8^2) in this context to explain the proportion of the observed score variance explained by the true score variance. If r^2 were erroneously used in this context, mathematically and conceptually, it would represent $(\sigma_T^2/\sigma_X^2)^2$ rather than the reliability (σ_T^2/σ_X^2).

Application VI: Validation

Validation can be viewed as an inquiry process pertaining to the accuracy of an interpretation or inference based on scores of a measure. A validity coefficient, often indexed by Pearson's r, reflects the degree of relatedness between inferences made about an event and the actual event. For instance, a corporate CEO infers employees' morale after downsizing on the basis of employees' responses on a job satisfaction inventory. The degree of the relationship between the inference of the job satisfaction score and the actual morale provides evidence of validity about the inventory. It should be emphasized that validity is not about a test itself. Instead, the validity of a test is concerned with how reasonable an inference is. Even a previously validated measure (e.g., a ruler) can be invalid if the inference (e.g., intelligence) resulting from the measure is erroneous.

While validating the above job satisfaction inventory, according to some theories, we may hypothesize positive relationships with measures of sense of responsibility, job commitment, satisfaction with pay, and relationship with one's supervisor, but we would hypothesize negative relationships with measures of intention to quit the job, feelings of frustration, anxiety at work, sabotage, and anger at work. The hypothesized correlations between job satisfaction and the other measures could be used to provide evidence of criterion-oriented validation about the inventory. The other job satisfaction measures, as well as the inventory presumed to assess the same construct, are expected to be positively related among one another. Furthermore, their relationships should be stronger than with scales measuring constructs other than job satisfaction. In other words, by conducting null hypothesis tests of equality between two dependent correlations, the sizes of these intercorrelations should be stronger than those found from the above criterion-oriented validation approach. The above findings would also provide evidence of convergence (Campbell & Fiske, 1959), as well as construct validation about the inventory.

The above correlations can be further summarized in the weblike network depicted in Figure 4.1. The signs (+) and (−) indicate the relationships of the job satisfaction inventory with other measures. In addition, the thickness of the lines reflects the strength of the relationships compared to others. This weblike network, also referred to as a nomological network (Cronbach & Meehl, 1955), represents a cluster of hypotheses, which provides a means of confirming or disconfirming the construct of interest. We should stress here that statistics only provide clues about the nature of the phenomenon. The validity of a measure should be evaluated according to the accumulated evidence from a complete nomological network.

As examples such as the above have shown, there are a variety of applications of Pearson's r that make this statistic useful for both researchers and practitioners. However, it is also important to

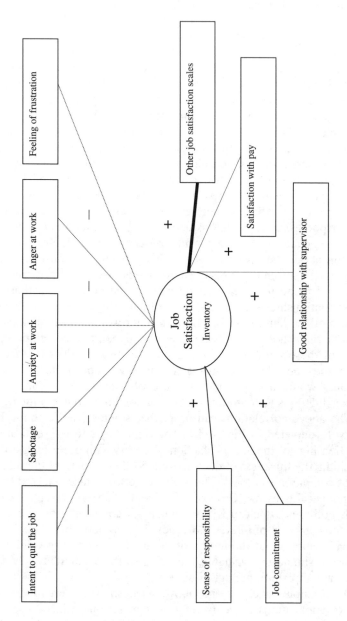

Figure 4.1. Demonstration of a Nomological Network About the Job Satisfaction Inventory

recognize the factors that affect the size and the interpretation of Pearson's r, which is the purpose of the next chapter.

5. FACTORS AFFECTING THE SIZE AND INTERPRETATION OF PEARSON'S r

In this chapter, we will discuss the factors that may affect the size, as well as the interpretation, of Pearson's r. These factors include shapes of distributions, sample sizes, outliers, restriction of range, aggregate samples, ecological inference, random error of measurement, and correlations with third variables.

Shapes of Distributions

Earlier, we mentioned that the possible range of correlation coefficients varies from −1 to 1. In this section, we will elaborate on that statement and note that this is true only when the distributions of X and Y are symmetrical and have the same form or shape (e.g., uniform distributions, normal distributions, U-shaped distributions). Although the null hypothesis test of $\rho = 0$ is robust to violations of normality, as described in Chapter 2, the maximum value of $|r|$ would be less than 1 if the distributions of X and Y had different shapes (e.g., if one were normally distributed and the other skewed). This is the reason the maximum value of $|r_{pb}|$ or $|\phi|$ tends to be less than 1.

Given that both distributions do not share the same form, increases in X will not always be accompanied by increases in Y (i.e., a case of a positive relationship) nor will increases in X always be paired with decreases in Y (i.e., a case of a negative relationship). As a result, the maximum value of $|r|$ will always be less than 1 with these distributions. The less similar the shape between both distributions, the smaller the maximum value (Carroll, 1961). Readers who are interested in estimating the maximum value under different shapes of distributions can refer to Carroll's seminal article (pp. 369–370).

Compared to the above example, the maximum value of Pearson's r can be +1 if both distributions are skewed to the same degree. However, it would then be impossible to obtain a correlation of −1. When the distributions of X and Y have the same skewed forms, there is a possibility that the values of X and Y for each pair will increase or decrease together. As a result, it is possible to obtain a correlation of $+1$. In contrast, increases (or decreases) in X cannot be paired with decreases (or increases) in Y with the same skewed distributions. Therefore, it is not possible to obtain a correlation of -1. Similarly, there is a possibility that the maximum value of Pearson's r reaches -1 but not $+1$ if both distributions are skewed toward the opposite directions, but with the same degree of skewness. In sum, the shapes of the distributions set the limit of Pearson's r, holding other factors constant.

Sample Size

The size of Pearson's r, as well as its precision in estimating the population correlation, ρ, tends to be affected by the sample size, particularly when the sample is small. Recall from Chapter 2 that the standard error for Pearson's r, $[(1 - \rho^2)^2/n]^{1/2}$, increases when the sample size is small. As a result, sample correlations poorly estimate the population correlation when the sample size is small. For example, when the sample size is 20, about 95% of the correlation coefficients will fall between -0.47 and 0.47, even though $\rho = 0$. In contrast, approximately 95% of the correlation coefficients will fall between -0.20 and 0.20 when the sample size is 102.

According to Wishart (1931), the expected value of r^2 when $\rho = 0$, $E(r^2)$, is a function of $1/(n-1)$. For instance, $E(r^2) = 1$ when there are two subjects in a sample. This example essentially shows that, whatever the two points, (x_1, y_1) and (x_2, y_2), they will determine a line. In other words, a perfect correlation based on any two cases can be obtained without a surprise, even though the population correlation can be any other value. In sum, when sample sizes are small, the expected values of r^2 tend to be relatively larger than 0, resulting from a capitalization on chance. Readers should be cognizant of this when interpreting Pearson's r based on a small sample size.

Outliers

Outliers are extreme values in the data, which may drastically affect Pearson's r, particularly when the sample size is small. Outliers can be found in one of two variables or both. Figure 5.1 is a scatterplot

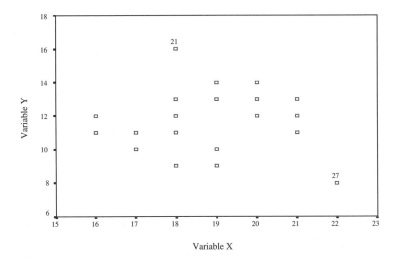

Figure 5.1. Scatterplot for Variable Y and Variable X

that shows the relationship ($r = 0.04$) between variable X and variable Y based on 27 cases. Case 27 in Figure 5.1 is an outlier and the correlation between X and Y would be 0.26 if case 27 were removed. If both cases 21 and 27 were removed, the correlation would move upward to 0.37. As can be seen from this example, the existence of presumed outliers in a small sample can easily affect either the size or the direction of Pearson's r. In general, a relatively large sample is less affected by outliers.

Restriction of Range

The correlation between two variables can also be affected by the restricted range of scores on one variable, or the other, or both. Scores can be restricted at one of two ends, both ends, or in the middle range of a distribution. There are many reasons that scores can be restricted. For example, measurement instruments may not be sensitive enough to capture the characteristics of the variables. In addition, people generally do not want to answer certain sensitive questions on topics such as alcohol or drug use. Furthermore, the distribution of an attribute in a population may be truly positively or negatively skewed. Under certain circumstances, job applicants may not admit if they have taken office supplies from work, nor will they endorse neurotic items on a neuroticism trait scale. As a result, the majority of responses to these scales will fall into the lower end of the distribution. Similarly, most people may feel positive about their lives, and the majority of the scores will then occur at the higher end of life satisfaction scales.

Range restriction could also occur when researchers select a relatively homogeneous sample for their studies. This type of selection is sometimes referred to as "incidental selection" (Glass & Hopkins, 1996). Homogeneity of the sample refers to the fact that all subjects share some common characteristics (e.g., personality, educational background, religion, geological location, etc.). In other words, they are indirectly "restricted" on some third variables, and they are much more alike on these background variables compared to a random sample. For example, if a third variable, such as mathematics major, is related to intelligence and/or calculus performance, the correlation between intelligence and calculus performance in the mathematics major sample tends to be different from that of a random sample.

The size of the correlation can either increase or decrease contingent upon the nature of the data, although it tends to decrease if either end of the measure is restricted or if the sample is homogeneous. In either case, range restriction tends to increase the standard error of the sampling distribution of Pearson's r, which, in turn, decreases the precision of estimating the population ρ from a sample r (Auguinis & Whitehead, 1997), as well as inflating the Type II error regarding the null hypothesis testing of $\rho = 0$.

If the assumption of a bivariate normal distribution is met, a correlation between variables X and Y under the unrestricted condition can be estimated by using the following correction formula:

$$\frac{r_r^2\left(\frac{s_u}{s_r}\right)^2}{1 + r_r^2\left(\frac{s_u}{s_r}\right)^2 - r_r^2} = \hat{r}_u^2,$$

where $\hat{r}_u$ is the estimated sample correlation under the unrestricted condition, r_r is the sample correlation under the restricted condition, s_u is the sample standard deviation of X under the unrestricted condition, and s_r is the sample standard deviation of X under the restricted condition.

Examining the correction formula, three conclusions can be made: (1) $\hat{r}_u > r_r$ if $s_u/s_r > 1$, (2) $\hat{r}_u < r_r$ if $s_u/s_r < 1$, and (3) $\hat{r}_u = r_r$ if $s_u/s_r = 1$.

A measure with the full range of scores tends to show more variation (i.e., larger variance) than the same measure with scores restricted in the lower or higher ends of the distribution. Because $s_u/s_r > 1$, the magnitude of a correlation in an unrestricted sample tends to be greater than that in a restricted sample according to the formula. The scatterplot in Figure 5.2a depicts the full range of scores for aggression and anger on the basis of 132 cases. The correlation coefficient between anger and aggression is 0.50, and the standard deviation of anger is 6.52. If the 52 cases with a low level of anger are removed from the original sample, a restriction of range occurs in the lower end, as depicted in Figure 5.2b, and the standard deviation of anger becomes 4.32. The correlation coefficient between anger and aggression also drops to 0.23.

A well-known scenario pertaining to this problem is the small correlation between graduate GRE and GPA. This value is often misleading because scores are restricted to the higher end on GREs and GPAs, with individuals scoring low on the GRE and having low GPAs not usually admitted and unavailable for study. Therefore, the correlation between GRE and graduate GPA tends to be lower than predicted.

A similar practical example is often discussed in terms of using personnel selection tests to predict employee performance. In practice, one or more valid personnel tests (e.g., the tests show significantly positive relationships with job performance) are used to select job applicants who pass the tests. Because the correlations between the personnel test and job performance are rarely obtained from all job applicants, the correlations tend to be smaller than expected. Suppose the standard deviation of the personnel selection test is 25 from a group of job applicants who are hired (i.e., the restricted group), and 50 from a group of job applicants (the unrestricted group). Although the correlation between the personnel selection test and job performance in the restricted group is 0.3, the estimated correlation turns out to be 0.53 should all applicants be hired:

$$\hat{r}_u^2 = \frac{(0.3)^2(50/25)^2}{1+(0.3)^2(50/25)^2-(0.3)^2} = 0.28 \quad \text{and} \quad \hat{r}_u = 0.53.$$

Returning to the previous example, if the 54 cases with a moderate level of anger are removed from the sample described in Figure 5.2a,

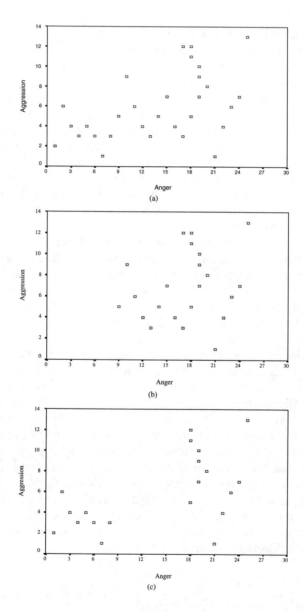

Figure 5.2. (a) Scatterplot for Anger and Aggression Without Ranges of Restriction. (b) Scatterplot for Anger and Aggression with Ranges of Restriction in the Lower End. (c) Scatterplot for Anger and Aggression With Ranges of Restriction in the Middle Range

a restriction of range occurs in the middle range, as depicted in Figure 5.2c. The correlation coefficient between anger and aggression in this restricted sample actually goes up to 0.63. By removing the middle range of scores, the variation in the restricted scores (e.g., a standard deviation of 7.95 for the measure of anger in Figure 5.2c) actually increases, compared to that of the full range of scores (e.g., a standard deviation of 6.52 for the same measure of anger in Figure 5.2a). Therefore, the size of the correlation in the restricted sample is likely greater than that in the unrestricted sample.

Another example of this problem can be found in what is referred to as extreme-group design. For instance, a political researcher investigates if there is any relationship between attitude toward social security and charity donation behavior. First, the researcher recruits people with either very positive or very negative attitudes about the social security system. In the results, the researcher reports a positive correlation of 0.5 between amount of charity donation and attitude. This extreme-group design provides higher statistical power, resulting from an increase in greater variation than the results of a design that recruits people with all levels of attitude. Consequently, it helps the researcher to find a stronger relationship between charity donation and attitude, even though the size of the true relationship could be smaller.

Suppose the standard deviation of the attitude is 10 in the group formed by the extreme-group design, and 5 in an unrestricted group. According to the correction formula, the correlation between attitude and charity donation in the unrestricted group is estimated at 0.28:

$$\hat{r}_u^2 = \frac{(0.5)^2(5/10)^2}{1+(0.5)^2(5/10)^2-(0.5)^2} = 0.08 \quad \text{and} \quad \hat{r}_u = 0.28.$$

Nonlinearity

As we have noted before, Pearson's r between two variables can be meaningfully interpreted only if the nature of the relationship is linear. If the relationship is not linear, then Pearson's r is not an appropriate index to describe the relationship because it could mask the true relationship. Figures 5.3a and 5.3b depict two different nonlinear relationships between X and Y. Both figures clearly show some form of relationship between X and Y, but both relationships cannot

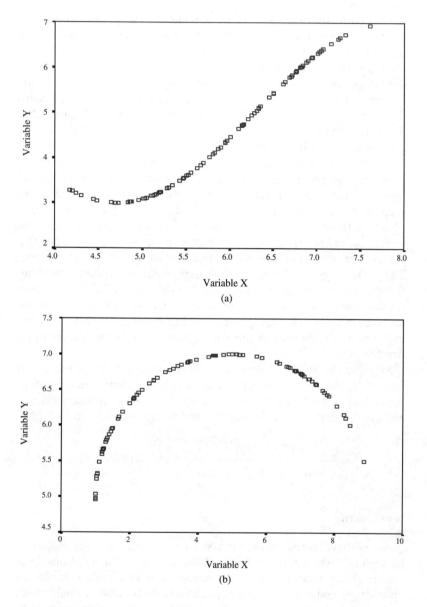

Figure 5.3. (a) Scatterplot for X and Y With a Nonlinear Relationship. (b) Scatterplot for X and Y With a Nonlinear (Curvilinear) Relationship

be described by a general linear function. In Figure 5.3a, an increase in X is accompanied by a decrease in Y initially. After X passes a point (i.e., when $X = 5$), an increase in X is accompanied by an increase in Y. In contrast, Figure 5.3b shows that an increase in X is initially accompanied by an increase in Y. After Y reaches the highest point of the diagram, an increase in X is accompanied by a decrease in Y. Both examples demonstrate some form of association between X and Y. However, it would be misleading to attempt to describe the above nonlinear relationships using Pearson's r. We recommend that readers first visually examine the relationship between two variables via a scatterplot. Should a nonlinear pattern occur, readers can either transform the data or employ some advanced approaches, such as polynominal regression (Bobko, 1995; Pedhazur, 1973).

Aggregate Samples

The size of Pearson's r can also be affected when it is calculated on the basis of a combination of multiple samples. For example, assume a school district wishes to examine if there is any positive relationship between state competency test performance and district competency test performance. The calculated correlation, based on 300 students from the three schools (A, B, and C), is -0.89. The school administrators are perplexed with this unexpected finding. Examining the scatterplot of each school in Figure 5.4a, the administrators can actually observe the trend of a positive relationship between the two test scores. Indeed, the correlation of each school ranges from 0.57 to 0.58. The reason a negative relationship is unexpectedly found may be attributed to the aggregation of the three samples. If one views these three groups as one single group, the resulting scatterplot would clearly show a negative pattern between the two tests. Another hypothetical example depicted in Figure 5.4b shows a near-zero correlation between cognitive ability and emotional intelligence found for 300 survey respondents from three different countries. However, the correlation coefficient turns into 0.98 if it is calculated by combining the three sets of samples together. It is clearly seen from Figure 5.4b that there is no relationship between cognitive ability and emotional intelligence in each country. However, the artificial positive relationship appears when the three samples are aggregated.

A more well known phenomenon, referred to as Simpson's paradox, also shows that relationships between dichotomous variables X

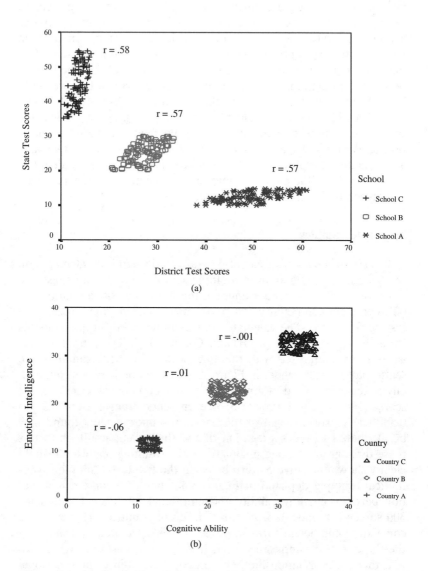

Figure 5.4. (a) Scatterplots for District Test Scores and State Test Scores Across Three Schools. (b) Scatterplots for Cognitive Ability and Emotional Intelligence Across Three Countries

(e.g., success or failure) and Y (e.g., male or female) for two combined samples (e.g., public and private schools) can be quite different from that of either sample. An example of this phenomenon is provided by the hypothetical data presented in Table 5.1, pertaining to students' admission at two universities within a state. Examining the admission rate for each university, both universities have demonstrated higher admission rates for female applicants (0.85 and 0.31, respectively) than for male applicants (0.79 and 0.18, respectively). However, the admission rate turns out to be higher for male applicants (0.69) than for female applicants (0.61) if we aggregate the results across the two universities.

The data in Table 5.1 provide the ϕ value for the individual, as well as the aggregate of the universities, in order to demonstrate the discrepant results at both the descriptive and the inferential levels of data analysis. According to the coding frames described in Table 5.1, a positive relationship suggests that female applicants are accepted more often than male applicants, and significant positive correlations are found for each university (0.07 and 0.13, respectively). In contrast, a significant negative correlation is found for the aggregate data (-0.07). It should be noted that the paradoxical result is attributed to the nature of the data (i.e., the different proportions of male or female applicants between the two universities). Simpson's paradox is not a contrived or manipulated finding, and this bewilderingly real-life statistical phenomenon has been reported in the literature.

The above illustration suggests that correlation coefficients that are calculated based on a combination of multiple samples will likely

TABLE 5.1
Example of Simpson's Paradox: Relationship Between
Gender and Admission

	Aggregate Sample		University A		University B	
	Male (0)	Female (1)	Male (0)	Female (1)	Male (0)	Female (1)
Admit (1)	4700	3600	4500	2800	200	800
Reject (0)	2100	2300	1200	500	900	1800
Admission rate	0.67	0.61	0.79	0.85	0.18	0.31
ϕ coefficient	-0.08[a]		0.07[a]		0.13[a]	

NOTE: People who are admitted are coded as 1 and people who are rejected are coded as 0. Males are coded as 0 and females are coded as 1.
a. $p < .001$, two-tailed.

provide misinformation as to the actual relationships. As suggested by Cohen and Cohen (1983), Rosenthal (1991), and Strube (1988), researchers should first examine if the correlations of multiple samples come from the same population by conducting a test of homogeneity

$$\chi^2 = \sum (n_k - 3)z_k^2 - \frac{\left(\sum (n_k - 3)z_k\right)^2}{\sum (n_k - 3)},$$

which was described in Chapter 2. If the test of homogeneity suggests those correlations are similar (i.e., belong to the same population), a weighted average

$$\bar{z} = \frac{(n_1 - 3)z_1 + (n_2 - 3)z_2 + \cdots + (n_k - 3)z_k}{(n_1 - 3) + (n_2 - 3) + \cdots + (n_k - 3)} \quad \text{and} \quad \bar{r} = \frac{e^{2\bar{z}_r} - 1}{e^{2\bar{z}_r} + 1}$$

can be employed to estimate the relationship. Should the average of a set of correlations derived from a sample (e.g., $r_{12}, r_{34}, r_{56}, r_{78}$) be calculated, the above equations can also be applied. It would be inappropriate to use

$$\bar{r} = \frac{(n_1 - 3)r_1 + (n_2 - 3)r_2 + \cdots + (n_k - 3)r_k}{(n_1 - 3) + (n_2 - 3) + \cdots + (n_k - 3)}$$

because it tends to underestimate to the average of a set of correlations.

If the test of homogeneity suggests those correlations are significantly different from one another, possible factors that are responsible for the differences should be explored or investigated. For instance, Carsten and Spector (1987) reported discrepancies among studies pertaining to the correlations between job satisfaction and turnover. They hypothesized that unemployment rates may be responsible for the different relationships. Employees who are not satisfied with their jobs tend to leave their jobs when there are ample job opportunities. However, the relationship is weakened when the unemployment rates increase. Dissatisfied employees would continue to stay in their jobs because there are few jobs available in the market. This illustrates, once again, the importance of sample characteristics when calculating and interpreting Pearson's r.

Ecological Inference

So far, we have discussed how Pearson's r is calculated based on individual subjects, even when discussing the topic of aggregate studies. In addition to treating individuals as the unit of analysis, researchers often study relationships among characteristics based on different units of analysis. For example, considering nations as the unit of analysis, a public policy staff in the United Nations could examine the relationship between the amount of welfare aid and the number of welfare recipients in the world. Viewing states as the unit of analysis, a transportation researcher could assess the relationship between highway speed limit and fatal auto accidents in the United States. Occupational health researchers could assess associations between demanding job characteristics and cardiovascular disease, while using each job as the unit of analysis.

These above examples all demonstrate the extended uses of Pearson's r. However, illogical or nonsensical conclusions from the findings of the above examples would appear *if* researchers attempt to infer the correlation from one level of units (e.g., schools) to another level of units (e.g., individual students). Robinson (1950) pointed out that conventional statistical methods (e.g., analysis of variance, multiple regression, or correlation) calculated on the basis of aggregate units do not reveal the same information that is obtained from individual units. Robinson actually demonstrated how discrepant results could occur when relationships between two variables are obtained from two different levels. He reported a correlation of 0.12 between whether respondents are Americans or not and the ability to read at the individual level, yet also revealed a correlation of -0.53 between the percentage of Americans and the percentage of people who were able to read at the state level. The challenge of exercising ecological inference is that the true relationship at the individual level could very likely be the reverse of the observed correlation based on the aggregate data (King, 1997). If we use the correlation derived from the aggregate data (e.g., a relationship between demanding job characteristics and cardiovascular disease at the job level) to infer the relationship at the individual level (e.g., a relationship between perceived job characteristics and blood pressure), we may be committing the notorious mistake often referred to as the ecological fallacy.

How can the correlation measured at the individual level differ from that obtained based on the aggregate data? This statistical challenge may be attributed to two major types of problems: aggregation bias and basic statistical problems (King, 1997). Aggregation bias occurs because important information is lost when individual level data are aggregated. For instance, employees under the same job title do not necessarily experience similar amounts of job pressure or cardiovascular disease. When studying the relationship between job pressure and percentage of heart disease across jobs, it may be very different from the relationship between job pressure and cardiovascular symptoms reported at the individual level. Regarding the basic statistical problems, King illustrates that ecological data often exhibit strong heteroscedasticity (e.g., variations of Y values that are different across different values of X) that is not captured by most widely used statistical models such as regression. Readers who are interested in various methods to verify ecological data should refer to King (1997).

Measurement Error

Random error of measurement (e.g., fatigue of test-takers) is another extremely important, but often neglected factor, which can decrease the relationship between variables. We have stressed the importance of using valid and reliable measures in science (and not only in the social sciences) in Chapter 4. If there is a large amount of random error in the measures, those measures become much less reliable. Imagine if we used unreliable measures in theory development or in practice: How much confidence could we have about the implications of the theories or applications?

How exactly does the random error affect the size of Pearson's r? The size of the correlation for true scores of X and Y varies as a function of the reliabilities of both variables, as well as the correlation of the observed scores of X and Y, as follows:

$$r_{T_X T_Y} = \frac{r_{O_X O_Y}}{\sqrt{r_{XX'} r_{YY'}}}.$$

- $r_{T_X T_Y}$ is the sample correlation between true scores of X and Y. In other words, it is the sample correlation between the perfectly reliable variables of X and Y.

- $r_{O_X O_Y}$ is the sample correlation between observed scores of X and Y. In other words, it is the sample correlation between the variables of X and Y, and neither measure is perfectly reliable.
- $r_{XX'}$ is the sample reliability of the measure X, ranging from 0 to 1.
- $r_{YY'}$ is the sample reliability of the measure Y, ranging from 0 to 1.

The above formula is referred to as the correction for unreliability. Holding $r_{T_X T_Y}$ constant, the less reliable the measures of X and Y (i.e., the more random error in measures), the smaller $r_{O_X O_Y}$ is. Put another way, $r_{T_X T_Y}$ is always greater than $r_{O_X O_Y}$ as long as either measure of X or Y is not perfectly reliable. The value of $r_{O_X O_Y}$ approaches the size of $r_{T_X T_Y}$ when measures of X and Y become perfectly reliable. Suppose the correlation between patient satisfaction after surgery and pain intensity is -0.2. Both patient satisfaction and pain intensity are self-reported measures with coefficient alphas (which is one type of internal consistency reliability estimate) of 0.7 and 0.6. Applying the above equation, the correction for unreliability ($r_{T_X T_Y}$) yields

$$r_{T_X T_Y} = \frac{r_{O_X O_Y}}{\sqrt{r_{XX'} r_{YY'}}} = \frac{-0.2}{\sqrt{0.7 \times 0.6}} = -0.31.$$

In other words, the relationship between patient satisfaction after surgery and pain intensity would have been stronger if both measures were perfectly reliable.

Although the above equation is quite handy in terms of correcting for unreliability, its application should be employed or interpreted with caution. We have previously introduced different reliability estimates (e.g., test-retest reliability) that gauge the effects of certain random errors (e.g., random errors that occur during a lapse of time). It is often unclear which appropriate reliability estimates should be chosen to represent both $r_{XX'}$ and $r_{YY'}$. Therefore, the size of a correlation corrected for unreliability will vary, contingent upon the choice of the reliability estimate. It does not seem justifiable to calculate a correlation corrected for unreliability merely based on available reliability estimates.

Third Variables

Often, two variables are statistically related, but, in fact, there is no true causal link between them. This relationship is considered to be a spurious or illusory relationship. How are two variables unrelated to each other, yet statistically related? The spurious relationship between two variables is often attributed to their relationships with one or more third variables. For instance, a positive relationship between age and job satisfaction is often reported in the literature. Could it be possible that the relationship is spurious resulting from their relationship to a third variable, such as job tenure? Research has shown that people who are satisfied with their job stay longer in a company (i.e., have a longer tenure). Therefore, job satisfaction is likely to affect tenure as shown in Figure 5.5a (indicated by the single-arrow solid line with a positive sign). It is also often found that employees who have longer tenure tend to be older (i.e., a positive relationship), although no assumption is made here about the causal relationship between tenure and age (shown by the double-arrow solid line with a positive sign). According to the above relational patterns, a positive relationship between age and job satisfaction (shown by the double-arrow dotted line) can be observed, even though the true relationship may be null.

A spurious relationship can also be observed when a third variable is simultaneously related to two other unrelated variables. For instance, a researcher reported a negative relationship between a standardized verbal test score and body weight in a university sample. There does not seem to be any theoretical reason why body weight is negatively associated with verbal performance, but it is possible that female students generally perform better in verbal tests and also weigh less than male students, as illustrated in Figure 5.5b. As shown in this figure, the relationships of gender with verbal scores and weight are depicted by two double arrow lines, in conjunction with a positive and a negative sign, respectively. Assuming the hypothetical model is viable, the observed negative relationship between verbal score and weight (shown by the dotted line) can be attributed solely to gender.

The above examples illustrate why a true null relationship can turn into a spurious relationship from a conceptual viewpoint. Statistically, the possible ranges of correlation between X and Y, when a third variable Z exists, can be written as

$$r_{xy} = r_{xz}r_{yz} \pm \sqrt{1 - r_{xz}^2 - r_{yz}^2 + (r_{xz}^2 r_{yz}^2)}$$

(McNemar, 1969). Suppose the relationships between job satisfaction and tenure and between tenure and age are 0.2 and 0.5, respectively.

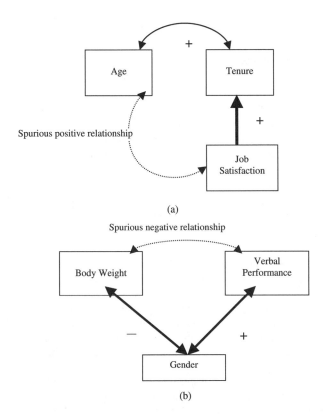

Figure 5.5. (a) Hypothetical Spurious Relationship Between Job Satisfaction and Age When Job Satisfaction Affects Tenure. (b) Hypothetical Spurious Relationship Between Verbal Score and Weight When Gender is Related to Verbal Performance and Body Weight

Following the above equation, the correlation between job satisfaction and age can range from −0.75 to 0.95, even though the hypothetical correlation is 0. The above equation further shows that a genuine relationship can be influenced by a third variable in either direction (i.e., an increase or decrease).

If a spurious relationship is assumed to exist (implications for which will be discussed in detail later), a genuine relationship between variables that is due to one or more additional variables can be examined by using various statistical control procedures (e.g., hierarchical regression analysis, analysis of covariance, or partial correlation). We will focus on the discussion of the first-order partial correlation, because it statistically controls only one variable. If two or more variables are controlled, the second-order or higher-order partial correlation can be obtained via a multiple regression approach.

A first-order partial correlation refers to a relationship between X and Y after the effect of a third variable, Z, is removed (i.e., statistically controlled). Under the assumption that Z is the *only* variable that affects variables X and Y, and that Z is *not* affected by either X or Y, the first-order partial correlation can be considered as the *genuine* correlation (Simon, 1954), and the relationship without controlling for Z is considered spurious. The underlying removal process of the first-order partial correlation is described below, using the example shown in Table 5.2.

1. Each individual i score on Y, Y_i, can be described by a linear function of Z_i, which is an individual i score on Z. This linear function, derived from the least squares solution, can be written as $Y_i = a_y + b_y(Z_i) + u_i$, where a_y and b_y are constants (e.g., 0.3 and 0.9 in Table 5.2) and u_i is the residual. Without getting into too much detail here, the least squares solution is just a method that minimizes the sum of the squared residual, $\sum_{i=1}^{n} u_i^2$, so that a_y and b_y can be obtained. The linear function suggests that the term $a_y + b_y(Z_i)$, is used to estimate Y_i. If $a_y + b_y(Z_i)$ overestimates Y_i, the u_i is negative; if $a_y + b_y(Z_i)$ underestimates Y_i, the u_i is positive; if $a_y + b_y(Z_i)$ accurately represents Y_i, the u_i become 0. In essence, u_i is the remaining component of Y_i that is not estimated by Z_i, and there is no relationship between Z and u as reported in Table 5.2.
2. Following the above procedure, each individual i score on X can be described by $X_i = a_x + b_x(Z_i) + v_i$, where a_x and b_x are constants

TABLE 5.2
Underlying Process of Removing a Third Variable, Z, in the First-Order Partial Correlation Between X and Y

X_i	Y_i	Z_i	$u_i = Y_i - 0.3 - 0.9(Z_i)$	$v_i = X_i - 1.2 - 0.6(Z_i)$
1	3	3	0	−2.0
2	1	2	−1.1	−0.4
3	2	1	0.8	1.2
4	4	4	0.1	0.4
5	5	5	0.2	0.8

NOTE: According to the least squares solution, $Y_i = 0.3 + 0.9(Z_i) + u_i$ and $X_i = 1.2 + 0.6(Z_i) + v_i$. $r_{XY} = 0.7$, $r_{XZ} = 0.6$, $r_{YZ} = 0.9$, $r_{uZ} = 0$, $r_{vZ} = 0$, and $r_{uv} = 0.46$.

(e.g., 1.2 and 0.6 in Table 5.2) and v_i is the residual. Likewise, v_i is the remaining component of X_i that is not estimated by Z_i. The correlation between v and Z is the same as that between u and Z, which is 0.

3. There are n pairs of (u_i, v_i) that represent n cases in a sample. Each pair of (u_i, v_i) is the component of X_i and Y_i that is not estimated by Z_i. Therefore, the correlation between u and $v(r_{uv})$, 0.46, reflects the relationship between X and Y after the effect of Z is removed, or the effect of Z is held constant (i.e., the first-order partial correlation between X and Y while controlling Z).

The first-order partial correlation between X and Y while controlling for Z, denoted as $r_{xy.z}$, can be directly obtained from the equation

$$r_{xy.z} = \frac{r_{xy} - r_{xz}r_{yz}}{\sqrt{1 - r_{xz}^2}\sqrt{1 - r_{yz}^2}},$$

without going through the cumbersome process described earlier. By substituting the correlations reported in Table 5.2 into the equation

$$r_{xy.z} = \frac{0.7 - (0.6)(0.9)}{\sqrt{1 - 0.6^2}\sqrt{1 - 0.9^2}} = 0.46,$$

we obtain the value of the first-order partial correlation, which is exactly the same as that of r_{uv}.

A test of the null hypothesis that $\rho_{xy.z} = 0$ can be conducted by a t test

$$t = \frac{r_{xy.z}}{\sqrt{1 - r_{xy.z}^2}}\sqrt{n - 3},$$

with the degrees of freedom of $(n - 3)^{1/2}$. Following the previous example, the observed t value of 0.73 derived from $0.46/(1 - 0.46^2)^{1/2}(5 - 3)^{1/2}$ is smaller than the critical t value, 4.30, $\alpha = 0.05$, two-tailed (refer to Appendix 1). Therefore, we conclude that we fail to reject the null hypothesis that $\rho_{xy.z} = 0$.

In contrast to the effect of measurement error that decreases the size of Pearson's r, unreliable measures may *increase, decrease*, or even change the *sign* of a partial correlation (Cohen & Cohen, 1983). There are four variations that can be used to correct the effect of unreliability on the first-order partial correlation: correcting unreliable X (or Y), correcting unreliable X and Y, correcting unreliable X, Y, and Z, and correcting unreliable Z only.

While only correcting either unreliable X or unreliable Y for $r_{xy.z}$, we can follow

$$r_{T_xO_y.O_z} = \frac{r_{O_xO_y} - r_{O_xO_z}r_{O_yO_z}}{\sqrt{(r_{XX'} - r_{O_xO_z}^2)(1 - r_{O_yO_z}^2)}} \quad \text{or}$$

$$r_{O_xT_y.O_z} = \frac{r_{O_xO_y} - r_{O_xO_z}r_{O_yO_z}}{\sqrt{(r_{YY'} - r_{O_yO_z}^2)(1 - r_{O_xO_z}^2)}}.$$

While only correcting unreliable X and Y for $r_{xy.z}$, we can follow

$$r_{T_xT_y.O_z} = \frac{r_{O_xO_y} - r_{O_xO_z}r_{O_yO_z}}{\sqrt{(r_{XX'} - r_{O_xO_z}^2)(r_{YY'} - r_{O_yO_z}^2)}}$$

While correcting unreliable X, Y, and Z for $r_{xy.z}$, we can follow

$$r_{T_xT_y.T_z} = \frac{r_{O_xO_y}r_{ZZ'} - r_{O_xO_z}r_{O_yO_z}}{\sqrt{(r_{ZZ'}r_{XX'} - r_{O_xO_z}^2)(r_{ZZ'}r_{YY'} - r_{O_yO_z}^2)}}.$$

While only correcting unreliable Z for $r_{xy.z}$, we can follow

$$r_{O_xO_y.T_z} = \frac{r_{O_xO_y}r_{ZZ'} - r_{O_xO_z}r_{O_yO_z}}{\sqrt{(r_{ZZ'} - r_{O_xO_z}^2)(r_{ZZ'} - r_{O_yO_z}^2)}}.$$

- $r_{T_xT_y.T_z}$ is the first-order partial correlation when all measures are perfectly reliable.
- $r_{T_xT_y.O_z}$ is the first-order partial correlation when measures of both X and Y are perfectly reliable.
- $r_{T_xO_y.O_z}, r_{O_xT_y.O_z}$, and $r_{O_xO_y.T_z}$ are the first-order partial correlations when the measure X, the measure Y, and the measure Z are perfectly reliable.
- $r_{O_xO_y}, r_{O_yO_z}$, and $r_{O_xO_z}$ are the zero-order correlations between observed scores of X and Y, X and Z, as well as Y and Z.
- $r_{XX'}, r_{YY'}$, and $r_{ZZ'}$ are the reliabilities of the measures X, Y, and Z.

If $r_{XX'} = 0.60$, $r_{O_x O_y} = 0.5$, $r_{O_x O_z} = 0.6$, and $r_{O_y O_z} = 0.7$, according to the above formulas, $r_{xy.z} = 0.14$ and $r_{T_x O_y.O_z} = 0.23$. This is an example that shows how measurement error can decrease the sample partial correlation. In contrast, if $r_{ZZ'} = 0.60$, $r_{O_x O_y} = 0.5$, $r_{O_x O_z} = 0.6$, and $r_{O_y O_z} = 0.7$, we will obtain $r_{xy.z} = 0.14$ and $r_{O_x O_y.T_z} = -0.74$, respectively. In this example, measurement error changes the sign of the partial correlation. Furthermore, measurement error would increase the size of a partial correlation when $r_{ZZ'} = 0.70$, $r_{O_x O_y} = 0.5$, $r_{O_x O_z} = 0.7$, and $r_{O_y O_z} = 0.5$. It can be seen from the formulas that the size of $r_{xy.z}(0.24)$ is greater than that of $r_{O_x O_y.T_z}(0)$.

Similar to the previous note regarding corrections for unreliability, the above formulas should be used with extreme caution. Different reliability estimates for the measures X, Y, and Z may lead to different inferences about the sizes of the partial correlation.

Olkin and Finn (1995) have provided a statistical test to examine if there is any difference between a zero-order correlation (r_{xy}) and a first-order partial correlation ($r_{xy.z}$). Because the process of conducting this statistical test is quite complicated, and the test is not available in the conventional canned programs, we have provided an SPSS® matrix program in Appendix 4. Readers can easily modify it for other matrix programs, such as SAS/IML®. The first section in Appendix 4 is the program, and the second section is the output. In the first section, users only input r_{xy}, r_{xz}, r_{yz}, and the sample size (e.g., -0.25578, -0.10498, 0.30986, and 110 in the example) into the line highlighted by Point 4-1. Make sure to leave at least one space between each data entry. The actual output consists of four numerical values, $r_{xy}, r_{xy.z}$, the difference between r_{xy} and $r_{xy.z}$, and an observed z value, respectively. If the observed z value is either greater than 1.96 or smaller than -1.96, ρ_{xy} is significantly different from $\rho_{xy.z}$ at $\alpha = 0.05$, two-tailed. As shown in the example, the observed z statistic (in absolute value) is smaller than 1.96. Therefore, the data fail to reject the null hypothesis that $\rho_{xy} = \rho_{xy.z}$.

Statistical control techniques such as the partial correlation are probably the most common methodologies exercised in contemporary social science research. For instance, a researcher examines a hypothesized model that variable X causes Z and Z causes Y. It is the simplest mediation model often observed in the social science literature. Within the model, variable Z is viewed as the factor that mediates the effect of variable X on variable Y. If the model is correct, the relationship between X and Y will decrease to 0 or a trivial size when the effect of Z is statistically removed. In other words, $r_{xy.z}$ is predicted to be close to 0.

The most frequent application of a statistical control in correlational analyses is to remove the effect of a presumed confounding or nuisance variable. If researchers believe the relationship between X and Y is confounded or contaminated by a nuisance variable Z (i.e., a third variable), a first-order partial correlation or other similar methodology can be applied. After controlling for the third variable, Z, $r_{xy.z}$ is predicted to be reduced, or close to 0, if r_{xy} is solely affected by Z.

Although the techniques are extremely easy to use and their practice is often taken for granted by most social scientists, potential misuses and erroneous inferences from statistical control cannot be overlooked. As Meehl (1971) warned, "...statistical manipulations cannot provide an automatic 'inference-machine,' but the tendency in social science is to treat control of nuisance variables in that way" (p. 147). Pedhazur (1973) has also pointed out that "Controlling variables without regard to the theoretical considerations...may amount to a distortion of reality and result in misleading or meaningless results" (p. 110).

Arguably, many variables are interrelated to some extent in the social sciences. It is not surprising that the size of a first-order partial correlation is often smaller than its correspondent zero-order correlation. Furthermore, even though a first-order partial correlation is "significantly" smaller than its correspondent zero-order correlation (as shown by applying Olkin and Finn's methodology described earlier), it is more difficult than researchers imagine to "prove" the effect of a third variable. We will use a controversial topic below to illustrate the concerns raised by Meehl (1971) and Pedhazur (1973).

In the life stress or job stress literature, self-reported results pertaining to relationships between stressful events or stressors (e.g., layoff, death of family member) and strains (e.g., depression or symptoms) are often viewed as spurious, resulting from the personality trait of neuroticism, which is a disposition to frequently experience negative emotions across situations and time. If the neuroticism trait is responsible for the stressor-strain relationship as shown in Figure 5.6a, the partial correlation between stressor and strain while controlling for the neuroticism trait should be much smaller than the correspondent zero-order correlation. Accepting the above assumption, some researchers have made the suggestion to statistically control for the

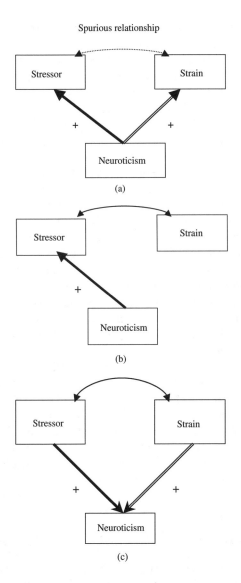

Spurious relationship

(a)

(b)

(c)

Figure 5.6. (a) Neuroticism Trait as a Third Variable That is Responsible for the Stressor-Strain Relationship. (b) Substantive Role of Neuroticism Trait in the Stressor-Strain Relationship: Neuroticism Trait Increases Stressful Incidents. (c) Substantive Role of Neuroticism Trait in the Stressor-Strain Relationship: Either Stressful Incidents or Strains Increase Neuroticism Trait neuroticism trait in conducting life stress or job stress surveys (see the review by Spector, Zapf, Chen, & Frese, 2000).

However, the neuroticism trait can be viewed as an important variable instead of a confounding variable. For example, people with a high neuroticism trait may have a tendency to be involved in conflict with others and, in turn, encounter more stressful incidents, as shown in Figure 5.6b. It could also very likely be, as illustrated in Figure 5.6c, that the experience of these stressful events (e.g., layoff, death of family member) or strains (e.g., depression or frustration) affect how people experience or see the world through a darkened lens.

Whatever the reasons the stress-strain relationship occurs, both models depicted in Figures 5.6b and 5.6c clearly suggest that the neuroticism trait is not a confounding variable. It should be stressed that the partial correlation between stressor and strain (while controlling for the neuroticism trait) based on both models is exactly the same as that based on the model in Figure 5.6a. These examples also demonstrate that the assumption of a third variable can never be substantiated by examining the reduction in a partial correlation. Because of potential misinterpretations and erroneous inferences from a partial correlation, readers should use any form of statistical control methodology with extreme caution.

Recognizing cautions such as these, as well as other factors that affect the size and interpretation of Pearson's r, is important in utilizing this statistic in a useful and effective manner. Recall from earlier chapters that there are also certain assumptions that must be met when using most versions of Pearson's r. There are, however, variations that will extend the usefulness of the correlation to situations in which those assumptions cannot be met, such as the nonparametric correlations described in the next chapter.

6. OTHER USEFUL NONPARAMETRIC CORRELATIONS

Most of the correlational statistics that we have presented in this monograph are considered to be parametric statistics. As mentioned in an earlier chapter, the distinction between parametric and nonparametric mainly results from whether population parameters (e.g., population correlation, ρ) are estimated, as well as whether certain assumptions (e.g., bivariate normal distribution) are met. In general, a nonparametric correlation requires fewer assumptions and does not attempt to estimate population parameters.

We have already discussed two nonparametric correlations, ϕ and r_{rank}, in Chapter 2. The former is used to measure the relationship between variables that are both dichotomous, and the latter is applied when assessing the relationship between two ordinal variables. In this final chapter, we will introduce seven additional nonparametric correlations: the C coefficient, Cramér's V coefficient, Kendall's τ coefficients (τ and τ_b), Stuart's τ_c coefficient, Goodman and Kruskal's γ coefficient, and Kendall's partial rank-order correlation, $\tau_{XY.Z}$. These indexes can also be used either as descriptive statistics or as inferential statistics.

C and Cramér's V Coefficients

To assess the association between two multichotomous variables, Cramér's V coefficient is preferred over the χ^2 statistic or contingency coefficient, C. To appreciate its advantages, however, a discussion of the χ^2 statistic and the contingency coefficient C is also needed. Recall that we briefly described the mathematical relationship between χ^2 and ϕ in Chapter 3, expressed as $\chi^2 = n\phi^2$, when both variables are dichotomous variables. In addition to handling dichotomous variables, the χ^2 statistic can also assess independence between two multichotomous variables.

Let us use the following example to demonstrate how to apply the χ^2 test of independence. Suppose a marketing researcher wants to find out if there is an association between choice of exterior paint color and advertisement media. In this experiment, people were exposed to one of three advertisement media (TV, newspaper, and Internet) about exterior paints of a particular brand name, and then, as potential consumers, they were asked to choose which one of three colors (white, brown, and blue) they preferred. Using information provided by 124 consumers on the three colors and the three media, the researcher created a 3×3 contingency table shown in Table 6.1. The χ^2 test of independence can be examined by

$$\chi^2 = \sum_{i=1}^{r} \sum_{j=1}^{c} \frac{(O_{ij} - E_{ij})^2}{E_{ij}}, \qquad df = (r-1)(c-1),$$

TABLE 6.1

3 × 3 Contingency Table Between Paint Colors and
Advertisement Media

	White	*Brown*	*Blue*	*Marginal Total*
Newspaper	$13 = O_{11}$	$10 = O_{12}$	$9 = O_{13}$	32
TV	$10 = O_{21}$	$35 = O_{22}$	$13 = O_{23}$	58
Internet	$15 = O_{31}$	$11 = O_{32}$	$8 = O_{33}$	34
Marginal total	38	56	30	

where r and c represent the number of rows and columns in the contingency table, O_{ij} is the observed cases in the ith row of the jth column, and E_{ij} is the expected cases in the ith row of the jth column when the null hypothesis is true (i.e., independence between two variables). E_{ij} can be computed by averaging the product of two marginal totals common to a particular cell in the contingency table.

According to the data described in Table 6.1, the researcher obtains

$$E_{11} = \frac{32 \times 38}{124} = 9.81, \qquad E_{12} = \frac{32 \times 56}{124} = 14.45,$$

$$E_{13} = \frac{32 \times 30}{124} = 7.7, \qquad E_{21} = \frac{58 \times 38}{124} = 17.77,$$

$$E_{22} = \frac{58 \times 56}{124} = 26.19, \qquad E_{23} = \frac{58 \times 30}{124} = 14.03,$$

$$E_{31} = \frac{34 \times 38}{124} = 10.42, \qquad E_{32} = \frac{34 \times 56}{124} = 15.35,$$

$$E_{33} = \frac{34 \times 30}{124} = 8.23.$$

Substituting each E_{ij} value into the equation

$$\chi^2 = \frac{(13 - 9.81)^2}{9.81} + \frac{(10 - 14.45)^2}{14.45} + \cdots + \frac{(11 - 15.35)^2}{15.35} + \frac{(8 - 8.23)^2}{8.23}$$
$$= 12.31.$$

According to the α of 0.05 and df of 4 in Appendix 2, the critical χ^2 value is 9.49, which is smaller than the observed χ^2 value. Therefore, the researcher concludes there is an association between paint color and advertisement medium. However, the observed χ^2 value does not reflect the strength of the association between these variables.

To express the strength of the association similar to the conventional correlation indexes, the contingency coefficient, C, can be applied, where

$$C = \sqrt{\frac{\chi^2}{n + \chi^2}}.$$

Substituting the sample size, n, and the observed χ^2 value, the researcher obtains

$$C = \sqrt{\frac{12.31}{124 + 12.31}} = 0.3.$$

This index suggests the association between paint color and medium is 0.3, which is significantly different from 0.

The C coefficient has been widely applied to assess an association between two unordered qualitative variables (Siegel & Castellan, 1988). However, the C coefficient cannot be unity even when there is a perfect association, because its upper limit is a function of the categories in the rows and columns. When the number of columns (c) and rows (r) is the same, the C coefficient equals $\sqrt{(c-1)/c}$ if there is a perfect association. For example, in the case of a 3×3 contingency table, the maximum value of the C coefficient is $\sqrt{(3-1)/3}$ or 0.82. Because the upper limit of the C coefficient depends on c and r, any two C coefficients are not comparable unless the two contingency tables have the same number of rows and columns.

To resolve the above first limitation, Cramér's V coefficient becomes the preferred choice. Cramér's V coefficient reflects the ratio of an observed statistic to its maximum statistic. As a result, it can range from 0 to 1. The computation formula is expressed as

$$V = \sqrt{\frac{\chi^2}{n \times [\min(r, c) - 1]}},$$

where $\min(r, c)$ is the smallest number of rows or columns in the contingency table. Substituting the previous data, the researcher obtains

$$V = \sqrt{\frac{12.31}{124 \times (3-1)}} = 0.22.$$

Similar to the C coefficient, any two V coefficients are not comparable unless the values of $\min(r, c)$ in both contingency tables are the same.

Kendall's τ Coefficient

Kendall's τ coefficient, a rival of r_{rank}, assesses the relationship between two ordinal variables. According to Kendall and Gibbons (1990), any two pairs of rank (X_i, Y_i) and (X_j, Y_j) are concordant if $Y_i < Y_j$ when $X_i < X_j$, or if $Y_i > Y_j$ when $X_i > X_j$, or if $(X_i - X_j)(Y_i - Y_j) > 0$. Similarly, any two pairs of rank (X_i, Y_i) and (X_j, Y_j) are discordant if $Y_i < Y_j$ when $X_i > X_j$, or if $Y_i > Y_j$ when $X_i < X_j$, or if $(X_i - X_j)(Y_i - Y_j) < 0$.

Let P be the number of concordant pairs and let Q be the number of discordant pairs. Based on n subjects to be ranked, there are $n(n-1)/2$ possible comparisons between any two pairs of rank (X_i, Y_i) and (X_j, Y_j), which is also equal to the sum of P and Q.

Conceptually, Kendall's τ coefficient is designed to assess the proportion of discrepancy between concordant pairs and discordant pairs, which can be expressed by

$$\tau = \frac{P - Q}{n(n-1)/2} \quad \text{or} \quad \tau = \frac{2(P - Q)}{n(n-1)}.$$

The sign of $(P - Q)$ determines the direction of a relationship. In other words, a positive relationship occurs when the value of $(P - Q)$ is positive, and a negative relationship appears when the value of $(P - Q)$ is negative. Similar to r_{rank}, Kendall's τ coefficient can range from -1 (a perfect negative relationship when $P = 0$) to 1 (a perfect positive relationship when $Q = 0$).

An example of the use of this statistic is provided by a situation in which two supervisors (X and Y) rank 10 employees (1 through 10) according to their job performance, with "1" as the lowest rank and "10" as the highest rank. To calculate Kendall's τ, first we order supervisor X's rankings of 10 employees so that $X_i < X_j$ for all $i < j$. After that, we list the correspondent rankings from supervisor Y. Note that the order of rankings from supervisor Y is mixed. The ranking results of two supervisors are presented in Table 6.2. Next, we need to determine the number of concordances ($Y_i < Y_j$ for all $i < j$)

TABLE 6.2
Ranks of 10 Employees on Job Performance by
Two Supervisors

Employee	Supervisor X	Supervisor Y	P	Q
1	$X_1 = 1$	$Y_1 = 6$	4	5
2	$X_2 = 2$	$Y_2 = 4$	5	3
3	$X_3 = 3$	$Y_3 = 2$	6	1
4	$X_4 = 4$	$Y_4 = 3$	5	1
5	$X_5 = 5$	$Y_5 = 1$	5	0
6	$X_6 = 6$	$Y_6 = 5$	4	0
7	$X_7 = 7$	$Y_7 = 7$	3	0
8	$X_8 = 8$	$Y_8 = 9$	1	1
9	$X_9 = 9$	$Y_9 = 8$	1	0
10	$X_{10} = 10$	$Y_{10} = 10$	0	0
Σ			34	11

and discordances ($Y_i > Y_j$ for all $i < j$) from each employee, start-ing with the first employee. The first employee is compared to the other nine employees (i.e., 1st vs. 2nd, 1st vs. 3rd, ..., 1st vs. 10th). The number of concordances (i.e., the number of employees ranked above 6 by supervisor Y) is 4, and the number of discordances (i.e., the number of employees ranked below 6 by supervisor Y) is 5. The second employee is then compared to the eight remaining employ-ees (i.e., 2nd vs. 3rd, 2nd vs. 4th, ..., 2nd vs. 10th). The number of concordances (i.e., the number of the remaining employees ranked above 4 by supervisor Y) is 5, and the number of discordances (i.e., the number of the remaining employees ranked below 4 by supervi-sor Y) is 3. Following the same procedure, both P and Q for the remaining employees, respectively, can be obtained, and are reported in Table 6.2. Substituting the data into the above equation,

$$\tau = \frac{34 - 11}{10(10 - 1)/2} = 0.51,$$

a result that suggests that the probability of two supervisors ranking these employees in the same order (concordant ranks) is 0.51 higher than that of two supervisors ranking these employees in the reverse order (discordant ranks), if the employees are sampled randomly.

When the sample size is greater than 10, the null hypothesis test of $\tau = 0$ can be computed using a z test

$$z = \frac{\tau}{\frac{\sqrt{2(2n+5)}}{3\sqrt{n(n-1)}}}.$$

Should the sample size be smaller than 10, the special critical values reported by Kendall and Gibbons (1990, pp. 204–205) should be consulted. Note that neither SAS® nor SPSS® has taken the small sample size into consideration.

Kendall's τ_b and Stuart's τ_c Coefficients

If tied ranks exist within either supervisor X or supervisor Y, those tied ranks are not counted in calculating P and Q. As a result, the sum of P and Q will not equal $n(n-1)/2$, which, in turn, causes the maximum value of Kendall's τ coefficient to be less than 1. We see an example of this based on a modification of the above data and presented in Table 6.3. In this case, X_6 and X_7 are tied with a rank of 6.5; Y_2, Y_3, and Y_4 are tied with a rank of 3; and Y_8 and Y_9 are tied with a rank of 8.5. As shown in Table 6.3, for instance, the number of discordances for the second employee (i.e., the number of $Y_2 < 3$) is 1 because Y_3 and Y_4 are not counted in calculating Q. Because X_6 and X_7 are tied, the number of concordances for the sixth employee (i.e., the number of $Y_6 > 5$) is 3, because Y_7 is not counted in calculating P.

To handle the tied ranks, two modified coefficients, Kendall's τ_b and Stuart's τ_c can be used. Both coefficients are different in terms of how tied ranks are treated. Unlike τ_b, τ_c can attain 1 in absolute value when two variables do not have the same number of ranked categories:

$$\tau_b = \frac{P-Q}{\sqrt{\frac{n(n-1)}{2} - U}\sqrt{\frac{n(n-1)}{2} - V}}, \qquad \tau_c = \frac{2m(P-Q)}{n^2(m-1)}.$$

- $U = \frac{1}{2}\sum u(u-1)$, where u is the number of observations tied at any given X value.
- $V = \frac{1}{2}\sum v(v-1)$, where v is the number of observations tied at any given Y value.

TABLE 6.3

Ranks of 10 Employees on Job Performance by
Two Supervisors With Tied Ranks

Employee	Supervisor X	Supervisor Y	P	Q	$u(u-1)$	$v(v-1)$
1	$X_1 = 1$	$Y_1 = 6$	4	5		
2	$X_2 = 2$	$Y_2 = 3$	5	1		
3	$X_3 = 3$	$Y_3 = 3$	5	1		$3(3-1)$
4	$X_4 = 4$	$Y_4 = 3$	5	1		
5	$X_5 = 5$	$Y_5 = 1$	5	0		
6	$X_6 = 6.5$	$Y_6 = 5$	3	0	$2(2-1)$	
7	$X_7 = 6.5$	$Y_7 = 7$	3	0		
8	$X_8 = 8$	$Y_8 = 8.5$	1	0		$2(2-1)$
9	$X_9 = 9$	$Y_9 = 8.5$	1	0		
10	$X_{10} = 10$	$Y_{10} = 10$	0	0		
Σ			32	8	2	8

- m is the smaller number of ranked categories used by supervisors X and Y.
- n is the number of employees ranked by the supervisors.

Based on the data in Table 6.3, we obtain $U = \frac{1}{2}[2(2-1)] = 1$, $V = \frac{1}{2}[3(3-1) + 2(2-1)] = 4$, $m = 7$ (i.e., supervisor Y only used seven categories in ranking), and $n = 10$ (i.e., 10 employees were ranked by the two supervisors). Substituting the above data into the correspondent formulas, both correlations are calculated as follows:

$$\tau_b = \frac{32-8}{\sqrt{45-1}\sqrt{45-4}} = 0.565 \quad \text{and} \quad \tau_c = \frac{2 \times 7 \times (32-8)}{10^2(7-1)} = 0.56.$$

The absolute value of τ_c is always smaller than $|\tau_b|$, given $n \geq m$ (Gibbons, 1993). If there is no tied rank, both U and V equal 0 and m equals 10; therefore, both τ_b and τ_c will be reduced to τ. The null hypothesis test of both τ_b and τ_c can be conducted by using a t test. The correspondent approximate standard error is quite complex, and readers can refer to Kendall and Gibbons (1990).

To contrast Kendall's τ coefficient and r_{rank}, we can use the same data in Tables 6.2 and 6.3 to obtain $r_{\text{rank}} = 0.70$ and $r_{\text{rank}} = 0.72$, respectively. In general, $|r_{\text{rank}}|$ is larger than τ, τ_b, or τ_c in absolute value. When there is no tied rank, the relationship between τ and r_{rank}

can be described as $-1 \leq 3\tau - 2r_{\text{rank}} \leq 1$ (Gibbons, 1993). The differences between both indexes are attributed to both the different scales of the two indexes (d in r_{rank} and $P - Q$ in τ) and the weights that r_{rank} emphasizes (Kendall & Gibbons, 1990). It can be seen from the r_{rank} computation formula that r_{rank} gives more weight (i.e., d^2) to inversions of ranks that are farther apart. It is often observed that $|r_{\text{rank}}|$ is 50% higher than $|\tau|$. Consequently, Kendall's coefficients (τ or τ_b) and Stuart's τ_c cannot be directly compared to r_{rank}.

Goodman and Kruskal's γ Coefficient

Although Kendall's coefficients and r_{rank} assess the relationship between two ordinal measures, these statistics are less useful and less appropriate when there are many tied ranks (Siegel & Castellan, 1988). Under these circumstances, Goodman and Kruskal's γ becomes a useful candidate to calculate the relationship between two ordinal measures. Goodman and Kruskal's γ can be obtained by

$$\gamma = \frac{P - Q}{P + Q}$$

and can range from -1 to 1. The only difference among γ, τ_b, and τ_c is how tied ranks are corrected. When there are no ties (e.g., the data in Table 6.2), Goodman and Kruskal's γ is equivalent to the corresponding Kendall's τ. When there are ties (e.g., the data in Table 6.3), Goodman and Kruskal's γ (0.6) is greater than Kendall's τ_b (0.565) and τ_c (0.56). In fact, Goodman and Kruskal's γ is always greater than the correspondent Kendall's coefficients when ties exist (Gibbons, 1993).

In sum, the only difference between Goodman and Kruskal's γ and Kendall's τ_b or Stuart's τ_c is how the tied ranks are corrected in the denominator of both equations. The null hypothesis test for Goodman and Kruskal's γ requires special critical values, although it can be examined by the z test when the sample size is large.

All the nonparametric correlation indexes described in the previous sections can be easily calculated via the CROSSTABS or NONPAR CORR commands in SPSS®, as well as the CORR or FREQ procedures in SAS®.

Kendall's Partial Rank-Order Correlation, $\tau_{XY.Z}$

Similar to the Pearson partial correlation discussed in Chapter 5, we can also obtain Kendall's partial rank-order correlation, $\tau_{XY.Z}$. Suppose there are three ordinal variables, X, Y, and Z. The partial rank-order correlation between X and Y while controlling for Z can be calculated by

$$\tau_{XY.Z} = \frac{\tau_{XY} - \tau_{XZ}\tau_{YZ}}{\sqrt{1 - \tau_{XZ}^2}\sqrt{1 - \tau_{YZ}^2}}.$$

The sampling distribution of $\tau_{XY.Z}$ is not distributed as either the t or the z distribution. Therefore, the null hypothesis test of $\tau_{XY.Z} = 0$ relies on special critical values reported by Kendall and Gibbons (1990, p. 237).

As can be seen from the above examples, nonparametric tests can be used in a variety of situations to assess relationships between variables. The use of the nonparametric statistics described here can extend the repertoire of researchers beyond the limits of parametric statistics. Readers who would like to learn more about other nonparametric measures should consult Gibbons (1993).

APPENDIX 1

Table of Critical t Values

Degrees of Freedom	Two-Tailed		One-Tailed	
	$\alpha = 0.05$	$\alpha = 0.01$	$\alpha = 0.05$	$\alpha = 0.01$
1	12.71	63.66	6.31	31.82
2	4.30	9.92	2.92	6.96
3	3.18	5.84	2.35	4.54
4	2.78	4.60	2.13	3.75
5	2.57	4.03	2.02	3.36
6	2.45	3.71	1.94	3.14
7	2.36	3.50	1.89	3.00
8	2.31	3.36	1.86	2.90
9	2.26	3.25	1.83	2.82
10	2.23	3.17	1.81	2.76
11	2.20	3.11	1.80	2.72
12	2.18	3.05	1.78	2.68
13	2.16	3.01	1.77	2.65
14	2.14	2.98	1.76	2.62
15	2.13	2.95	1.75	2.60
16	2.12	2.92	1.75	2.58
17	2.11	2.90	1.74	2.57
18	2.10	2.88	1.73	2.55
19	2.09	2.86	1.73	2.54
20	2.09	2.85	1.72	2.53
21	2.08	2.83	1.72	2.52
22	2.07	2.82	1.72	2.51
23	2.07	2.81	1.71	2.50
24	2.06	2.80	1.71	2.49
25	2.06	2.79	1.71	2.49
26	2.06	2.78	1.71	2.48
27	2.05	2.77	1.70	2.47
28	2.05	2.76	1.70	2.47
29	2.05	2.76	1.70	2.46
30	2.04	2.75	1.70	2.46
40	2.02	2.70	1.68	2.42
50	2.01	2.68	1.68	2.40
60	2.00	2.66	1.67	2.39
70	1.99	2.65	1.67	2.38
80	1.99	2.64	1.66	2.37
90	1.99	2.63	1.66	2.37
100	1.98	2.63	1.66	2.36
110	1.98	2.62	1.66	2.36
120	1.98	2.62	1.66	2.36

APPENDIX 2

Table of Critical χ^2 Values

Degrees of Freedom	$\alpha = 0.05$	$\alpha = 0.025$	$\alpha = 0.01$
1	3.84	5.02	6.63
2	5.99	7.38	9.21
3	7.81	9.35	11.34
4	9.49	11.14	13.28
5	11.07	12.83	15.09
6	12.59	14.45	16.81
7	14.07	16.01	18.48
8	15.51	17.53	20.09
9	16.92	19.02	21.67
10	18.31	20.48	23.21
11	19.68	21.92	24.72
12	21.03	23.34	26.22
13	22.36	24.74	27.69
14	23.68	26.12	29.14
15	25.00	27.49	30.58
16	26.30	28.85	32.00
17	27.59	30.19	33.41
18	28.87	31.53	34.81
19	30.14	32.85	36.19
20	31.41	34.17	37.57
21	32.67	35.48	38.93
22	33.92	36.78	40.29
23	35.17	38.08	41.64
24	36.42	39.36	42.98
25	37.65	40.65	44.31
26	38.89	41.92	45.64
27	40.11	43.19	46.96
28	41.34	44.46	48.28
29	42.56	45.72	49.59
30	43.77	46.98	50.89
40	55.76	59.34	63.69
50	67.50	71.42	76.15
60	79.08	83.30	88.38
70	90.53	95.02	100.43
80	101.88	106.63	112.33
90	113.15	118.14	124.12
100	124.34	129.56	135.81
110	135.48	140.92	147.41
120	146.57	152.21	158.95

APPENDIX 3

SPSS Syntax and Output to Find the Ordinate, λ, of a Standardized
Normal Distribution at the Proportion of Subjects in Sample 2

SPSS Syntax

Data list free/prop.
Begin data.
.50 ◄──────────────── Enter proportion in this line
End data.
Compute z = probit(prop).
Compute lamda = 1/(sqrt(exp(z**2)*2*3.1415927)).
Format lamda (f7.6).
Print/ 'Proportion = ' prop '/ ' 'Ordinate of the
    proportion = ' lamda.
execute.

SPSS Output

Proportion = .50/Ordinate of the proportion = .398942

APPENDIX 4

SPSS Syntax and Output for Testing if a Zero-Order Correlation Is Different From a First-Order Partial Correlation

Syntax

```
data list free/rXY rXZ rYZ n.
begin data.
−0.25578      −0.10498      0.30986      110        ◄─── Point 4-1: your data are
end data.                                               entered in this line
matrix.
compute output = make(1,4,−99).
get M/file = *.
  compute the rXY = M(1,1).
  compute rXZ = M(1,2).
  compute rYZ = M(1,3).
  compute n = M(1,4).
  compute rXY_Z = (rXY − rXZ*rYZ)/sqrt((1 − rXZ**2)*(1 − rYZ**2)).
  compute a1 = 1 − sqrt((1 − rXZ**2)*(1 − rYZ**2)).
  compute a2 = (rXY*rXZ − rYZ)/(1 − rXZ**2).
  compute a3 = (rXY*rXZ − rXZ)/(1 − rXZ**2).
  compute a = {a1,a2,a3}.
  compute phi11 = (1 − rXY**2)**2.
  compute phi22 = (1 − rXZ**2)**2.
  compute phi33 = (1 − rYZ**2)**2.
  compute phi12 = (.5*(2*rYZ − rXY*rXZ)*(1 − rYZ**2-rXY**2-rXZ**2))
             + rYZ**3.
  compute phi13 = (.5*(2*rXZ − rXY*rYZ)*(1 − rYZ**2 − rXY**2 − rXZ**2))
             + rXZ**3.
  compute phi23 = (.5*(2*rXY − rXZ*rYZ)*(1 − rYZ**2 − rXY**2 − rXZ**2))
             + rXY**3.
  compute phi = {phi11, phi12, phi13; phi12, phi22, phi23; phi13, phi23, phi33}.
  compute phi = (1/n)*phi.
  compute aphia = a*phi*t(a).
  compute var = aphia/((1 − rXZ**2)*(1 − rYZ**2)).
  compute se = sqrt(var).
  compute d = rXY − rXY_Z.
  compute z = d/se.
  compute output(1,1) = rXY.
  compute output(1,2) = rXY_Z.
  compute output(1,3) = d.
  compute output(1,4) = z.
  print output.
end matrix.
```

Output

Run MATRIX procedure:

OUTPUT
−.2557800000 −.2361122906 −.0196677094 −.6041359397

-----END MATRIX-----

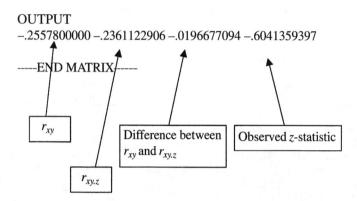

REFERENCES

ALLIGER, G. M., & JANAK, E. A. (1989). Kirpatrick's levels of training criteria: Thirty years later. *Personnel Psychology, 42,* 331–342.

ARONSON, E., ELLSWORTH, P. C., CARLSMITH, J. M., & GONZALES, M. H. (1990). *Methods of research in social psychology* (2nd ed.). New York: McGraw-Hill.

AUGUINIS, H., & WHITEHEAD, R. (1997). Sampling variance in the correlation coefficient under indirect range restriction: Implications for validity generalization. *Journal of Applied Psychology, 82,* 528–538.

BOBKO, P. (1995). *Correlation and regression: Principles and applications for industrial organizational psychology and management.* New York: McGraw-Hill.

BYERLY, H. C. (1973). *A primer of logic.* New York: Harper & Row.

CAMPBELL, D. T., & FISKE, D. W. (1959). Convergent and discriminant validation by the multitrait-multimethod matrix. *Psychological Bulletin, 56,* 81–105.

CARMINES, E. G., & ZELLER, R. A. (1979). *Reliability and validity assessment.* Newbury Park, CA: Sage.

CARROLL, J. B. (1961). The nature of the data, or how to choose a correlation coefficient. *Psychometrika, 26,* 347–372.

CARSTEN, J. M., & SPECTOR, P. E. (1987). Unemployment, job satisfaction, and employee turnover: A meta-analytic test of the Muchinsky model. *Journal of Applied Psychology, 72,* 374–381.

CASCIO, W. F. (1991). *Costing human resources: The financial impact of behavior in organizations* (3rd ed.). Boston: PWS-Kent.

COHEN, J. (1962). The statistical power of abnormal-social psychological research: A review. *Journal of Abnormal and Social Psychology, 65,* 145–153.

COHEN, J. (1988). *Statistical power analysis for the behavioral sciences* (2nd ed.). Hillsdale, NJ: Lawrence Erlbaum.

COHEN, J., & COHEN, P. (1983). *Applied multiple regression/correlation analysis for the behavioral sciences* (2nd ed.). Hillsdale, NJ: Lawrence Erlbaum.

COOK, T. D., & CAMPBELL, D. T. (1979). *Quasi-experimentation: Design and analysis issues for field settings.* Boston: Houghton Mifflin.

CRONBACH, L. J., & MEEHL, P. E. (1955). Construct validity in psychological tests. *Psychological Bulletin, 52,* 281–302.

DOWDY, S. M., & WEARDEN, S. (1991). *Statistics for research* (2nd ed.). New York: John Wiley.

EDGELL, S. E., & NOON, S. M. (1984). Effect of violation of normality on the *t* test of the correlation coefficient. *Psychological Bulletin, 95,* 576–583.

FISHER, R. A. (1921). On the "probable error" of a coefficient of correlation deduced from a small sample. *Metron, 1,* 1–32.

GIBBONS, J. D. (1993). *Nonparametric measures of association.* Sage University Paper Series on Quantitative Applications in the Social Sciences, 07-090. Newbury Park, CA: Sage.

GLASS, G. V., & HOPKINS, K. D. (1996). *Statistical methods in education and psychology* (3rd ed.). Boston: Allyn & Bacon.

94

HAYS, W. L. (1994). *Statistics* (5th ed.). New York: Harcourt Brace.

HOWELL, D. C. (1997). *Statistical methods for psychology* (4th ed.). Albany, NY: Wadsworth Publishing Company.

HUNTER, J. E., & SCHMIDT, F. L. (1990). *Methods of meta-analysis.* Newbury Park, CA: Sage.

JAMES, L. R., MULAIK, S. A., & BRETT, J. M. (1982). *Causal analysis: Assumptions, models and data.* Beverly Hills, CA: Sage.

KENDALL, M., & GIBBONS, J. D. (1990). *Rank correlation methods* (5th ed.). New York: Oxford University Press.

KING, G. (1997). *A solution to the ecological inference problem.* Princeton, NJ: Princeton University Press.

McNEMAR, Q. (1969). *Psychological statistics* (4th ed.). New York: John Wiley.

MEEHL, P. E. (1971). High school yearbooks: A reply to Schwarz. *Journal of Abnormal Psychology, 77,* 143–148.

MURPHY, K. R., & MYORS, B. (1998). *Statistical power analysis.* Hillsdale, NJ: Lawrence Erlbaum.

OLKIN, I., & FINN, J. D. (1995). Correlations redux. *Psychological Bulletin, 118,* 155–164.

PEARSON, K. (1957). *The grammar of science.* New York: Meridian Books. (Originally published, 1892.)

PEDHAZUR, E. J. (1973). *Multiple regression in behavioral research* (2nd ed.). New York: Holt, Rinehart & Winston.

PEDHAZUR, E. J., & SCHMELKIN, L. P. (1991). *Measurement, design, and analysis: An integrated approach.* Hillsdale, NJ: Lawrence Erlbaum.

ROBINSON, W. S. (1950). Ecological correlations and the behavior of individuals. *American Sociological Review, 15,* 351–357.

ROSENTHAL, R. (1991). *Meta-analytic procedures for social research.* Newbury Park, CA: Sage.

SEDLMEIER, P., & GIGERENZER, G. (1989). Do studies of statistical power have an effect on the power of studies? *Psychological Bulletin, 105,* 309–316.

SIEGEL, S., & CASTELLAN, N. J. (1988). *Nonparametric statistics for the behavioral sciences* (2nd ed.). New York: McGraw-Hill.

SIMON, H. A. (1954). Spurious correlation: A causal interpretation. *American Statistical Association Journal, September,* 467–479.

SPECTOR, P. E., ZAPF, D., CHEN, P. Y., & FRESE, M. (2000). Why negative affectivity should not be controlled in job stress research: Don't throw out the baby with the bath water. *Journal of Organizational Behavior, 21,* 79–95.

STEIGER, J. H. (1980). Tests for comparing elements of a correlation matrix. *Psychological Bulletin, 87,* 245–251.

STRUBE, M. (1988). Averaging correlation coefficients: Influence of heterogeneity and set size. *Journal of Applied Psychology, 73,* 559–568.

TRATTNER, M. H., & O'LEARY, B. S. (1980). Sample sizes for specified statistical power in testing for differential validity. *Journal of Applied Psychology, 65,* 127–134.

WHERRY, R. J., SR. (1984). *Contributions to correlational analysis.* New York: Academic Press.

WISHART, J. (1931). The mean and second moment coefficient of the multiple correlations coefficient in samples from a normal population. *Biometrika, 22,* 353–361.

ABOUT THE AUTHORS

PETER Y. CHEN (Ph.D., University of South Florida) is Associate Professor of Industrial/Organizational Psychology at Colorado State University. He was previously a research scientist at Liberty Mutual Research Center for Safety and Health and Associate Professor of Industrial/Organizational Psychology at Ohio University. His primary research interests are in occupational health, personality, performance evaluation, training, and methodology, and he has published articles pertaining to these areas in various journals, including *Journal of Applied Psychology, Journal of Management, Journal of Occupational Health Psychology, Journal of Organizational and Occupational Psychology, Journal of Organizational Behavior, Journal of Personality Assessment, International Journal of Human-Computer Interaction*, and *Group and Organization Management: An International Journal.*

PAULA M. POPOVICH (Ph.D., Michigan State University) is Associate Professor of Psychology at Ohio University. As an industrial and organizational psychologist, her research interests have included attitudes toward computer usage, as well as topics in organizational diversity, including sexual harassment and attitudes toward working with disabled persons. She has published papers on these and other topics in a number of journals, including *Academy of Management Review, Educational and Psychological Measurement, Journal of Applied Social Psychology, Journal of Psychology, Journal of Occupational Health Psychology, Perceptual and Motor Skills*, and *Training and Development Journal.*